W9-BGJ-991

MATTERS OF THE HEART

Devotions for Women

MATTERS OF THE HEART

Devotions for Women

JUANITA BYNUM

A STRANG COMPANY

Most STRANG COMMUNICATIONS/CHARISMA HOUSE/SILOAM products are available at special quantity discounts for bulk purchase for sales promotions, premiums, fund-raising and educational needs. For details, write Strang Communications/Charisma House/Siloam, 600 Rinehart Road, Lake Mary, Florida 32746, or telephone (407) 333-0600.

MATTERS OF THE HEART DEVOTIONS FOR WOMEN by Juanita Bynum
Published by Charisma House
A Strang Company
600 Rinehart Road
Lake Mary, Florida 32746
www.charismahouse.com

This book or parts thereof may not be reproduced in any form, stored in a retrieval system or transmitted in any form by any means—electronic, mechanical, photocopy, recording or otherwise—without prior written permission of the publisher, except as provided by United States of America copyright law.

Unless otherwise noted, Scripture quotations are from the Amplified Bible. Old Testament copyright © 1965, 1987 by the Zondervan Corporation. The Amplified New Testament copyright © 1954, 1958, 1987 by the Lockman Foundation.
Used by permission.

Scripture quotations marked KJV are from the King James Version of the Bible.

Scripture quotations marked NIV are from the Holy Bible, New International Version. Copyright © 1973, 1978, 1984, International Bible Society. Used by permission.

Scripture quotations marked NKJV are from the New King James Version of the Bible. Copyright © 1979, 1980, 1982 by Thomas Nelson Publishers. Used by permission.

Scripture quotations marked THE MESSAGE are from *The Message: The Bible in Contemporary English*, copyright © 1993, 1994, 1995, 1996, 2000, 2001, 2002. Used by permission of NavPress Publishing Group.

Cover design by Judith McKittrick
Interior design by Terry Clifton

Copyright © 2003 by Juanita Bynum
All rights reserved

Library of Congress Cataloging-in-Publication Data
Bynum, Juanita
  Matters of the heart devotions for women / Juanita Bynum.
      p. cm.
includes bibliographical references.
  ISBN 1-59185-229-3 (hardback)
  1. Christian women—Prayer books and devotions—English. I. Title.
242'.643—dc22

                                         2003017861
              03 04 05 06 07 — 87654321
              Printed in the United States of America

CONTENTS

SECTION TEN: CARING FOR THE NEW HEART

SECTION ELEVEN: PRAYER AND THE NEW HEART

INTRODUCTION

Are you ready to "get real" with God? Is your heart crying out for a deeper, more intimate walk with Him?

God is calling His church, His people, back to Him in this hour. Without realizing it, we have fallen into error—even while we have continued to do "good" things for God. We have tripped, stumbled and fallen in doing what He requires. But now, He is calling us to a radical change—a "surgical procedure" that will remove our old heart, which struggles to obey His will, and replace it with His new heart, a heart inclined to follow His ways.

The message of the new heart was a new one for me. I believed that I was saved, that I was serving God. But I had not realized that God was demanding a radical transformation—a complete heart transplant, and with it, a complete change in my life.

Beloved, God is calling for change from the inside out, whether you minister from the church platform, work in the nursery or sit in the pew. Receive and embrace His Word. Practice the power of prayer every day. Let go of religion. Let go of the past. Enter the new day!

Train me, God, to walk straight; then I'll follow your true path. Put me together, one heart and mind; then, undivided, I'll worship in joyful fear. From the bottom of my heart I thank you, dear Lord; I've never kept secret what you're up to. You've always been great toward me—what love!

—PSALM 86:11–13, THE MESSAGE

MATTERS
OF THE
HEART

SECTION

ONE

Devotions for Women

SPIRITUAL HEART DISEASE

I HAVE COME TO

THIS REALIZATION.

IF YOU LET THIS

WORD GO DEEP,

SO WILL YOU.

AM I REALLY SAVED?

I knew that I was saved—born and raised in the church for that matter—so why was God birthing this "new heart" message in me? Didn't He know to whom He was talking? I had grown up in the ministry and then moved on into my own full-time ministry, so I was used to the routine. I didn't realize it at that moment, but it was time for a change.

Does Jesus really live here? Am I sure, beyond the shadow of a doubt, that He lives in me?

I was not expecting to receive a "new heart" message. I felt that I had given my heart to God when I was converted, but somewhere along the way it had gone into a dormant state. I began to operate from my "works," not from my heart.

I had to be honest with myself and realize that my heart was not right. I had to ask, "*Am I really saved? Does Jesus really live here? Am I sure, beyond the shadow of a doubt, that He lives in me?* I do not have any doubt that He uses me . . . but does Jesus live here? Am I His?"

Hear this message that God gave to me. Sin and God cannot dwell in the same heart at the same time. Righteousness and unrighteousness cannot dwell in the same temple. I am talking about your heart. Hear me. You did not so receive Christ. Did you really get it?

The "new heart" was Jesus' greatest message. It is the Bible's greatest story. In all of Scripture, that with which God is most concerned is this vital truth—*the matters of the heart*.

The heart is deceitful above all things, and it is exceedingly perverse and corrupt and severely, mortally sick! Who can know it [perceive, understand, be acquainted with his own heart and mind]? I the Lord search the mind, I try the heart, even to give to every man according to his ways, according to the fruit of his doings.

—JEREMIAH 17:9–10

It's time to get real. It's time to change.

BECOMING MORE LIKE JESUS

Hear me. It is time to seek God like never before. It is time to fall down at the altar and ask Him to renew your heart. It is time to become more like Jesus, for real! "Church as usual" is over! It is time to take off the "old wineskin" and put on the "new man." (See Matthew 9:16–17; Colossians 3:9–10.)

God has been walking me through this process for several years.

> *"Church as usual" is over!*

As I began to write this book, I realized that I could only "birth" chapters as the Holy Spirit moved me—and say only what He had given me to say. So as you read on, understand that this is a work of the Spirit. God wants you to know that He is breathing a message through His prophet for this hour.

This birthing has been difficult, sometimes painful, so I know it will not be easy for you to read or to digest. Why? It is spiritual meat. It takes more energy to digest meat in the natural, and it is no different in the realm of the Spirit. You will have to work through the revelation, just as God led me to do. So take your time, chew every piece and let it go down deep—because by the time you finish, a new work will have begun inside you.

Joel 2:11–12 says:

> And the Lord utters His voice before His army, for His host is very great, and [they are] strong and powerful who execute [God's] word. For the day of the Lord is great and very terrible, and who can endure it? Therefore also now, says the Lord, turn and keep on coming to Me with all your heart, with fasting, with weeping, and with mourning [until every hindrance is removed and the broken fellowship is restored].

As you walk through this devotional, the Lord wants you to understand this purpose: that you would turn and keep on turning, and come and keep on coming—for in doing this, you will be transformed, and any broken fellowship with the Lord will be restored.

> *When you come looking for me, you'll find me. Yes, when you get serious about finding me and want it more than anything else, I'll make sure you won't be disappointed.*
> —JEREMIAH 29:13, THE MESSAGE

It is time to become more like Jesus—for real!

7

HEADING IN A NEW DIRECTION

Righteous one, God is calling you to turn! Get up, turn around and start walking in a new direction. Change is necessary for all of God's people. Whether you are a pastor, lay minister, church member or missionary, God wants you to "divide" this Word, first to yourself, and then to others.

> *I have come to this realization: If you let this Word go deep, so will you.*

God is calling us to get back up. We must realize that the church is only a jump-start. Truly living for God doesn't start until you leave the church and interject the message from the church into your lifestyle. We must understand that the church is where believers come to fellowship, but God's Word is made manifest outside the church.

Remember, the man that lay at the Beautiful Gate was begging for alms from men going into the sanctuary. Peter looked at him and said, "Silver and gold (money) I do not have; but what I do have, that I give to you" (Acts 3:6). He ended up finding his deliverance, healing and breakthrough! This means when people in the sanctuary really begin to take hold of the Word of the Lord—and are transformed by their new hearts—the *true riches* in their hearts can be made manifest in the world.

As you read, God will deposit something new inside you if you ask for it. Receive and embrace this Word. Receive this prophetic call, and God will bless, strengthen and guide you in the days to come. Your heart will begin to turn in a new direction . . . and, like me, you will know that you can never turn back.

It is time to let go of the past. Let go of religion. Let go of sin and anything that keeps you from drawing close to God and obeying His prophetic cry for this final hour.

Therefore if any man be in Christ, he is a new creature: old things are passed away; behold, all things are become new.
—2 CORINTHIANS 5:17, KJV

Church, as we have known it, is over. God is sounding the charge.

TAKE AN HONEST LOOK

If we are not careful, we can be doing a religious work and still be backslidden in our hearts. We can do this without realizing it, either because our works are so wonderful or because the responses our works are getting are so wonderful. We may even feel God's anointing and presence upon our works, which can, in itself, become a deception. How? Our works can be so good that we never stop to recheck our heart to see if it is found in right standing with God.

Our works can be so good that we never stop to recheck our heart to see if it is found in right standing with God.

Righteousness is ours. We must make sure that the past does not rob us of what already belongs to us. When we walk, looking back into our past, there is no way we can find the path of the Lord. We must understand: It is possible to be trapped in our own deception about who we are—enjoying our successes from the past and yet not being purified enough to see the future.

We must remember and understand the story of King Uzziah (2 Chron. 26). God gave him powerful victories, and then he became deceived. He arrogantly went into the temple to offer incense, which he was not appointed by God to do. *King Uzziah thought that because he had succeeded in life he had succeeded in God.* We must never get the two mixed up.

Regardless of everything I do—the preaching, the singing and all of the ministering—I am still human just like anyone else. Recently God told me, "I want you to turn off the music . . . turn off all the preaching tapes . . . be alone with yourself and see what comes out of your mind. Then you will know what state you are in. If you do this, you will be surprised what you hear yourself saying."

Thought patterns can emerge in your mind because it has to be transformed. But when all the stuff that goes on in your mind becomes a continuous rotation, and it comes out in your behavior, then are you really saved? Take an honest look at yourself, and ask God to reveal your true heart.

The heart is deceitful above all things, and it is exceedingly perverse and corrupt and severely, mortally sick! Who can know it [perceive, understand, be acquainted with his own heart and mind]? I the Lord search the mind, I try the heart, even to give to every man according to his ways, according to the fruit of his doings.
—JEREMIAH 17:9–10

 Ask God to reveal your true heart.

CHOOSE THE NEW HEART!

You may wonder what happened at the point of conversion when you came up to the altar to be saved from your sinful nature. Was your heart truly converted? What happens to your heart at the moment of repentance?

We can look at the example of King David, a man after God's own heart. When he reached his moment of repentance and asked God to forgive him for his sins, he said, "Create in me a clean heart, O God, and renew a right, persevering, and steadfast spirit within me" (Ps. 51:10). That is exactly what took place right at that moment you asked Him to forgive you of your sins. He created a clean heart in you and renewed a right spirit within you. Within your heart your spirit sits.

The only way your renewed mind can fail to come into harmony with your new heart is by your choice.

It is your "old mind" that keeps you functioning outside the will of God. Your mind needs to be transformed constantly by a process of renewing. When the renewed mind lines up with the conversion that is in your heart, you are a new creature—completely inside and out.

The only way your renewed mind can fail to come into harmony with your new heart is by your choice. You must choose whether to follow the stubborn habits that are stored in your memories or to submit to the wisdom that flows out of your new heart.

When the Word of the Lord says we are to be transformed by the renewing of our mind, it means *exercising* the mind and bringing it into obedience to the Word.

Now every athlete who goes into training conducts himself temperately and restricts himself in all things. They do it to win a wreath that will soon wither, but we [do it to receive a crown of eternal blessedness] that cannot wither. Therefore I do not run uncertainly (without definite aim). I do not box like one beating the air and striking without an adversary. But [like a boxer] I buffet my body [handle it roughly, discipline it by hardships] and subdue it, for fear that after proclaiming to others the Gospel and things pertaining to it, I myself should become unfit [not stand the test, be unapproved and rejected as a counterfeit].

—1 CORINTHIANS 9:25

If we do not bring our thought patterns under subjection to the Lord, during the time of testing—when we are tried—we will fail, revealing ourselves as counterfeits.

THE GREAT PRETENDERS

I want to make this clear. We must all come to a place where we either admit that we do not have a new heart or that we have mastered the act of salvation and become the great pretenders. Let me give you an example. Suppose someone tells you, "When you are saved, you are supposed to love Sister Watermelon." So you speak to Sister Watermelon and hug her; you do the saved "act," but in your heart, you cannot stand her.

We have taught each other to master the "church act."

What has happened to the church across the board is that we have become men pleasers. We have taught each other to master the "church act." Everybody looks saved; we know how to act saved; we know how to do saved stuff; and we know how to project saved. But our hearts are far from it— we are not even close. We are the great pretenders.

To all who fit into that category, one day Jesus will say: "You say you have cast out devils in My name and have healed the sick in My name—but begone from Me; I never knew you." (See Matthew 25:41.) Don't let Him say that to you!

What Jesus means is this: "I never had a relationship with YOU. You *worked* for Me, but I did not have a *relationship* with you."

When fellowship becomes your choice (rather than service),

you have received a portion from the Lord that can never be taken away from you—because no one can ever break your relationship with God. Many choose to work in the service of the Lord—*but Mary chose to have fellowship with the Lord.* She broke the cycle of works.

***

Now while they were on their way, it occurred that Jesus entered a certain village, and a woman named Martha received and welcomed Him into her house. And she had a sister named Mary, who seated herself at the Lord's feet and was listening to His teaching. But Martha [overly occupied and too busy] was distracted with much serving; and she came up to Him and said, Lord, is it nothing to You that my sister has left me to serve alone? Tell her then to help me [to lend a hand and do her part along with me]! But the Lord replied to her by saying, Martha, Martha, you are anxious and troubled about many things; there is need of only one or but a few good things. Mary has chosen the good portion [that which is to her advantage], which shall not be taken away from her.

—LUKE 10:38–42

***

A person who maintains the reins of his heart and controls the patterns of his mind impresses God.

MATTERS

SECTION

OF THE

TWO

HEART

Devotions for Women

WHY WE NEED A TRANSPLANT

When you say,
"I love You, Lord,"
but still walk
in your ways, then
you do not really
love the Lord.

THE "SO-CALLED" WALK WITH THE LORD

One day a gentleman suggested to me that people were looking for a God who was attainable and reachable. I asked myself, "Is God attainable?" I realized I could not answer that question.

I began to question God about this new heart. I felt strange, like some kind of cancer was eating away at me, something that I could not shake off. I had to come to terms with God and with myself.

When we pursue the image of perfection, we cannot strive to understand the heart of God.

When we pursue the image of perfection, we cannot strive to understand the heart of God. If we consistently paint a picture that everything is perfect, beautiful and wonderful—"You know you have reached God when you look like me...dress like me...walk and talk like me"—then we have totally missed God! We have become a group of people who constantly pursue an image—not God!

This takes me to the story of Naaman in the Book of Second Kings, chapter 5. Naaman was a great warrior who had a great image, but he had leprosy. God used a little slave girl who had been taken into his camp to usher in his healing. She told his wife, "I know a man who would heal him." Ultimately, Naaman had to swallow his pride, go down to the Jordan River and dip seven times (as the prophet Elisha had instructed him) to receive his healing. At that moment, above all the knowledge and understanding he had, he received a new understanding about the healing power of God.

So many times in our lives we get preoccupied with our problems and situations that have come upon us—and we don't know which way to turn. Yes, in reality, God is giving us a passageway (in disguise) to receive His understanding.

So who even comes close to being like God? To whom or what can you compare him?...Don't you know anything? Haven't you been listening? God doesn't come and go. God lasts.

—ISAIAH 40:18, 28, THE MESSAGE

He is giving us an opportunity to come out of religion and into relationship.

LIVING IN A "BRAIN WORLD"

We are all struggling in our own way, trying to make sure that we "do right" from our heart. Through my study, I discovered that this world has become a brain world. It functions from the activities of the brain, out of the intellect of our finite brains. We are consumed with brain knowledge, and because we are consumed with this knowledge, our lives are constantly being constructed and operated by the laws of the intellect. What that means is this: If you do me wrong, then my intellect (based on the information that I have gathered from you) reacts and says, "I am going to do you wrong."

The world has trained us to bypass our heart's conviction and to operate within the realm of our mind and emotions.

The brain teaches us how to scheme, lie, connive and manipulate. Here is the truth. God has put a spirit of conviction in our hearts, which corrects us when we do something wrong. The world, however, has trained us to bypass our heart's conviction and to operate within the realm of our mind and emotions. For this reason, we have a chaotic world.

This is also the reason why no one is seeking after God for a changed, new heart. We do not want to change; we only want to feel better—for the moment. In order to get eternal gratification, we have to give up something right now.

The mind is the place of argument because it has immediate access to the knowledge of this world. It always argues about what it feels it has accomplished through its own success—really, through the process of wickedness. Always remember, the mind defends *the now,* but the heart defends *the eternal.*

We're all like sheep who've wandered off and gotten lost.
We've all done our own thing, gone our own way. And God
has piled all our sins, everything we've done wrong, on him.
—Isaiah 53:6, The Message

In order to get eternal gratification, we have to give up something right now.

THE OLD HEART: A "PROFESSIONAL SINNER"

The Bible says that we are born in sin and shaped in iniquity (Ps. 51:5). We are born with an "old heart" nature that is already coated with the potential to do wrong. When we come into the world, our hearts are already shaped for this sin.

Iniquity is anything you do that God is not in. It is anything done against the will of God or against the laws or nature of God. If something is contrary to His character, it is iniquity. You have been shaped in that area by what society has taught you.

> *We are born with an "old heart" nature that is already coated with the potential to do wrong.*

Because your heart is composed of the potential to sin, your mind is gradually trained to become a professional sinner. When your heart and mind "match up" in the spirit, then you have the heart described in Jeremiah 17:9 as "desperately wicked" (KJV). It is desperately deceitful...who can know it? Who can understand the depths of that heart?

It took the disaster of 9/11 to bring a "seek" back into this country. It took this attack and the fear of ongoing terrorist attacks from another country to bring us to our knees. It took this incident to help us realize that in spite of all the cars, houses and everything we have, we need the Lord. Before 9/11, our hearts and minds had left the Lord. We were not seeking Him. When we walk with hearts that are "shaped in iniquity," hearts that are born in sin, seeking the Lord is not important in them. This kind of heart does not come with a "Yes, Lord" in it.

A heart that is provoked to pursue God out of fear and hurt is not the kind of heart that provokes us to eternal change. It is the kind of heart that pursues temporary relief. We saw examples of this after the 9/11 attacks. Churches were packed out every Sunday with people who seemed to be coming to the Lord. What was actually drawing them into God's house was fear and hurt. Since that time, statistics have proven that churches everywhere are back to the way things were before 9/11. People were pursuing God with *old hearts* that just needed a break.

Behold, I was brought forth in [a state of] iniquity; my mother was sinful who conceived me [and I too am sinful].
—PSALM 51:5

When we walk with hearts that are "shaped in iniquity," hearts that are born in sin, seeking the Lord is not important in them.

THE OLD HEART: A "SELFISH LOVER"

So how can this "old heart," which was "born in sin" and "shaped in iniquity," love God? Real love cannot come out of this heart. Only a *phileo* kind of love (which means the natural human affection, with its strong feeling, or sentiment) can come from a wicked heart. *Agape* love (unconditional and eternal) is never found in our "old hearts." The only way that you can truly love God is to love Him with the same love that He has given to you. It has to match in the third realm. You cannot love God from an earthly level, because God is eternal, and it can never work to love Him from an earthly perspective.

> *Agape love (unconditional and eternal) is never found in our "old hearts."*

Agape love could never be found in the "old heart" because it possesses the characteristics of eternal damnation. According to Christ, you can't really operate in *agape* until you can see the ugly and still love.

Loving God brings about a commitment to Him. When you love somebody, you are committed to him in every way. There is nothing that you will not do for someone you love. A real relationship with God enables you to walk in His commandments.

God wants to have a relationship with us, and not just when things are going wrong. He desires to have a relationship that touches every facet of our lives. Think about it. How would you feel if your friends and family members called only when there was an emergency? Any other time you didn't hear from them at all. This is how the Lord feels when He has made it possible for us to come into daily, hourly, minute-by-minute relationship with Him—and we don't. We must realize that He is concerned about every detail, every moment, of our lives.

And now, Israel, what does the Lord your God require of you but [reverently] to fear the Lord your God, [that is] to walk in all His ways and to love Him, and to serve the Lord your God with all your [mind and] heart and with your entire being.

—DEUTERONOMY 10:12

Loving God brings about a commitment to Him.

THE DECEPTION OF PROSPERITY

We must learn to deal with the deception of prosperity. We can find ourselves saying things like this: "I feel so much love for the Lord because of all the things He has blessed me with." Beware of the deception that can come with the prosperity of God's blessing upon our lives. God told the children of Israel:

> Remember every road that God led you on for those forty years in the wilderness, pushing you to your limits, testing you so that he would know what you were made of, whether you would keep his commandments or not.
>
> —DEUTERONOMY 8:2, THE MESSAGE

Beware of the deception that can come with the prosperity of God's blessing upon our lives.

God has allowed us to look upon the example of the children of Israel in the wilderness so that we could learn from their experiences. I believe that God has allowed not just the secular world but also the church to go the "way" that we have gone to prove to us that we really do not love Him. He has done this to "try" us and to see what is really in our hearts and minds. The problem we face today, which is a huge problem and a mighty task, is that we, God's people, must ask for a new heart.

Understand that believers must operate in the *ultimate*. We should have an ultimate love for the Lord when He is digging us out and chastising us.

> *Those whom I [dearly and tenderly] love, I tell their faults and convict and convince and reprove and chasten [I discipline and instruct them]. So be enthusiastic and in earnest and burning with zeal and repent [changing your mind and attitude].*
>
> —REVELATION 3:19

"How do I get back to God—simply God?"

THE DECEPTION OF RELIGION

King Solomon inherited the kingdom of his father, David, and was handed the plans of the tabernacle that David had earnestly desired to build. Yet in 1 Kings 11:3, we discover that "his wives turned away his heart" from God (NKJV). Even though he began his reign over Israel by seeking God's wisdom, and even though he built the temple of God, his kingdom became little more than a religious organization—and he lost his relationship with his Father God.

> *Like Solomon, we do not even realize that our hearts are being drawn away.*

Like Solomon, we do not even realize that our hearts are being drawn away. We may have walked closely with God in the past and, like Solomon, may have even prayed for His wisdom to guide our steps. Verse 9 goes on to tell us that God had already appeared to Solomon and commanded him that he should not go after other gods! However, Solomon did not do what the Lord had commanded. His disobedience kindled the anger of God:

> Therefore the Lord said to Solomon, Because you are doing this and have not kept My covenant and My statutes, which I have commanded you, I will surely rend the kingdom from you and will give it to your servant!
>
> —1 KINGS 11:11

This is a powerful revelation—one that carries great significance for us. God has been forewarning the church structure for many years, saying, "Get this thing together; get this thing in order. I want you to provoke My people to come after My heart, to provoke My people unto righteousness."

We in the church have considered ourselves to be "structured" and "mighty." We think that we have all of the answers. We have an appearance of God—but because we have not turned our hearts toward Him, we are leaving God with no other choice except to reach out, get the heathen and raise them up. They are the ones who have received the new heart.

I see right through your work. You have a reputation for vigor and zest, but you're dead, stone dead . . . Think of the gift you once had in your hands, the Message you heard with your ears—grasp it again and turn back to God.
　　　—REVELATION 3:1, 3, THE MESSAGE

We have an appearance of God—but because we have not turned our hearts toward Him, we are leaving God with no other choice except to reach out, get the heathen and raise them up.

MATTERS

SECTION

OF THE

THREE

HEART

Devotions for Women

IT'S AN INSIDE-OUT PROBLEM

THE HEART DETERMINES

WHETHER OR NOT

YOU ENTER

THE KINGDOM OF GOD.

THE "INSIDE-OUT" PROBLEM

The world—and part of the church—is crying out, but our problem always seems to be someone else's fault. Before you will see your own need, you must be confronted—just as I was—with the reality of what God is saying. The problem is not what is entering your life from external sources. It is not the fault of what is taking place around you. Those things that come at you from external sources are merely identifying with something that is already in your heart.

The heart determines whether or not you enter the kingdom of God.

If the outside problem finds a place of identification, a familiar spirit, inside you, then you absolutely, no doubt about it, need to be transformed. You need the new heart.

Why is the church in the position now of not realizing we need a new heart? Why do we feel that by getting our outward appearance "right," we are getting somewhere with God? It is because man looks outside, but God looks within—at the heart. It is our hearts that God is coming back for—nothing else. The heart—not the mind—determines whether or not you enter the kingdom of God.

We should not be concerned with outer things. We should focus on what is inside. When we get the "inside" to line up with

God's Word, we will change! God will give us a new heart, and this heart will begin to manifest on the outer man just as the old heart works from the inside out.

For the Lord sees not as man sees; for man looks on the out-ward appearance, but the Lord looks on the heart.
—1 Samuel 16:7

It is our hearts that God is coming back for—nothing else.

THE DECEITFUL HEART

What about our old heart? Is it simply a "poor, little, confused, messed-up heart"? We can begin to understand the condition of our old heart by taking a closer look at Jeremiah 17:9: "The heart is deceitful above all things, and it is exceedingly perverse and corrupt and severely, mortally sick! Who can know it [perceive, understand, be acquainted with his own heart and mind]?"

> *The most important thing is to have the new heart and to know that you know—you have it!*

There is a definition for the word *deceitful* in this verse that startled me—it also means, "to be unfaithful." The saddest fact about this heart—and again, shockingly so—is that it is "unfaithful." It can never be dedicated to God. It can never keep a commitment. Maybe this is the reason why people constantly move in and out of relationships, or why the divorce rate is so high. Perhaps it is the reason why so many children are living in orphanages, or why prostitution is rampant. Maybe it is even why there is such a lack of integrity in the body of Christ. This deceitful heart does not have what it takes to be faithful to anything—God or man.

An unfaithful heart hinders us from being blessed, because Proverbs 28:20 says, "A faithful man shall abound with blessings." This means you remain in a continual state of being blessed! You walk *continually* in the posture of blessing when your heart belongs to the Lord and His faithfulness is imparted and made manifest *in you*. It is through faithfulness that we walk in the *true blessings* of the Lord.

Who knows the depths of his heart to the degree that he can furnish this heart with the knowledge it will take to walk toward God? No man does. But God does—because pieces of it are everywhere and in every direction! He goes on in Jeremiah 17:10 (THE MESSAGE):

> But I, God, search the heart and examine the mind. I get to the heart of the human. I get to the root of things. I treat them as they really are, not as they pretend to be.

Yes, we have a real problem. But God has the solution—the new heart.

> *So turn around! Turn your backs on your rebellious living so that sin won't drag you down. Clean house. No more rebellions, please. Get a new heart! Get a new spirit . . . Make a clean break! Live!*
> —EZEKIEL 18:30–32, THE MESSAGE

This deceitful heart does not have what it takes to be faithful to anything—God or man.

THE ENEMY'S GROUND

How is the "evil one" able to snatch a Word that has been sown in someone's heart? He is familiar with the grounds. He (Satan) already knows that the Word is trying to penetrate that heart; he knows the base character of that heart does not have what it takes to absorb and to hold that Word. Satan has authority to do things according to the flesh because this ground belongs to him! He is the "prince of the power of the air" (Eph. 2:2). The worldly realm is his, but Satan has not been given authority over the spiritual realm. God warns that if you do not walk in the Spirit, your heart has become foreign ground.

When a believer walks in the Spirit, spiritual knowledge of all things is made accessible to him—which becomes pertinent to his cleansing.

> *Satan has authority to do things according to the flesh because this ground belongs to him!*

He withdraws not His eyes from the righteous (the upright in right standing with God); but He sets them forever with kings upon the throne, and they are exalted. And if they are bound in fetters [of adversity] and held by cords of afflic-tion, then He shows to them [the true character of] their

deeds and their transgressions, that they have acted arro-
gantly [with presumption and self-sufficiency]. He also
opens their ears to instruction and discipline, and com-
mands that they return from iniquity. If they obey and serve
Him, they shall spend their days in prosperity and their
years in pleasantness and joy. But if they obey not, they
shall perish by the sword [of God's destructive judgments],
and they shall die in ignorance of true knowledge.

—JOB 36:7–12

The earth realm is "legal" ground for
Satan. This is why believers must walk in
the Spirit.

ROCKY SOIL REPELS GOD'S WORD

The old heart is filled with rocky soil—soil that cannot be penetrated with the deep, life-transforming Word of God. People whose hearts are filled with rocky soil may welcome the Word of the Lord—even crave it—but because it cannot penetrate deep into their spirits, they settle for an artificial emotional response to God rather than being rooted and grounded in Him.

> *People whose hearts are filled with rocky soil settle for an artificial emotional response to God rather than being rooted and grounded in Him.*

Jesus talked about this rocky soil of the old heart and the response it brings: "The seed cast in the gravel—this is the person who hears and instantly responds with enthusiasm" (Matt. 13:20, THE MESSAGE).

Emotionalism—are you seeing the revelation? Many people hear the Word and "accept it with joy." You can see it every Sunday in the church. People hollering back at the preacher . . . shouting, "Amen, preach it" all over the church. "Yet . . . ," the Bible says:

> There is no soil of character, and so when the emotions wear off and some difficulty arrives, there is nothing to show for it.
> —MATTHEW 13:21, THE MESSAGE

God is describing people who hear the Word, but there is no real heart penetration. There is no depth to where His Word can be planted. It floats around in the "emotional" realm, and when something else "exciting" charges these emotions in a different way and direction, the first Word is canceled out. The emotions, which are fleshly, take precedence at that moment over the Word of God. The Word does not reside in this heart, and it cannot find a resting place.

Recognize the rocky soil of your old heart. Determine today to cast off your old heart with its rocky soil and allow the deep, penetrating Word of God to take root in your new heart so that you may be rooted and grounded in God.

A white-tailed deer drinks from the creek; I want to drink God, deep draughts of God. I'm thirsty for God-alive. I wonder, "Will I ever make it—arrive and drink in God's presence?"

—PSALM 42:1–2, THE MESSAGE

Allow the deep, penetrating Word of God to take root in your new heart.

THORNY SOIL CHOKES GOD'S WORD

The fruit of the Word of God at work in our lives cannot exist amidst the weeds that grow rampant in a life that has not received a new heart. If we want God's Word to take root and produce fruit in our lives, we must create an environment within our new hearts that is weed free.

> *If we want God's Word to take root and produce fruit in our lives, we must create an environment within our new hearts that is weed free.*

God is the Master Landscaper of our new hearts. The salvation garden He creates within our new hearts will prepare us not only to receive the Word, but also to be changed by it as we hear that Word and respond to it. The Bible tells us that once we have that new heart, we will be able both to hear the Word *and to act on it*: "Don't fool yourself into thinking that you are a listener when you are anything but, letting the Word go in one ear and out the other. *Act* on what you hear!" (James 1:22, THE MESSAGE).

People who do not have the "new heart" hear the truth but often fail to act upon it. They rationalize that truth and come up with every reason why "this is not what the Bible means." Their hearts are so filled with the world and the things of the world that they are deceived into thinking they have all they need.

Don't allow the "world and the pleasure and delight and glamour and deceitfulness of riches" to "choke and suffocate the Word" when God attempts to penetrate your heart with it. Don't let these "good" things choke the Word out of your heart! That is perversion.

For if anyone only listens to the Word without obeying it and being a doer of it, he is like a man who looks carefully at his [own] natural face in a mirror; for he thoughtfully observes himself, and then goes off and promptly forgets what he was like.

—JAMES 1:23–24

Don't allow the "world and the pleasure and delight and glamour and deceitfulness of riches" to "choke and suffocate the Word" when God attempts to penetrate your heart with it.

FRUITFUL SOIL EMBRACES GOD'S WORD

The person who is good soil has a converted heart. This person, who has received a new heart, has an "active" Word on the inside. "The seed cast on good earth is the person who hears and takes in the News, and then produces a harvest beyond his wildest dreams" (Matt. 13:23, THE MESSAGE).

When the Word takes up residence in this new heart, it operates with divine power and produces more fruit.

God's spoken Word comes alive and produces good fruit. This Word has the power to save and the power to keep. The penetrating Word is filled with power! It energizes your spirit, heart and soul as it accomplishes God's will. This Word can never be stagnated. It goes down into the intricate parts of the inner man and "dissects" everything it finds there. When the enemy comes in "like a flood," that Word knows how to swim. When the fire rages, that Word knows how to hold its breath. When the wind starts blowing, that Word is anchored. When the sun starts to blaze, that Word knows how to get in the shade—regardless of what life's temperature may be.

When the Word takes up residence in this heart, it operates with divine power and produces more fruit. This heart embraces the Word it has received and produces more than it has been given.

The Word that goes into a "new heart" is active. It "identifies" with the divine nature of God and multiplies.

⁂

For the Word that God speaks is alive and full of power [making it active, operative, energizing, and effective]; it is sharper than any two-edged sword, penetrating to the dividing line of the breath of life (soul) and [the immortal] spirit, and of joints and marrow [of the deepest parts of our nature], exposing and sifting and analyzing and judging the very thoughts and purposes of the heart. And not a creature exists that is concealed from His sight, but all things are open and exposed, naked and defenseless to the eyes of Him with Whom we have to do.

—HEBREWS 4:12–13

⁂

The penetrating Word is filled with power! It energizes your spirit, heart and soul as it accomplishes God's will.

SPIRITUAL LAZINESS

Be aware that spiritual laziness resides in your old heart. It may prevent you from "acting" upon the Word of God and seeking the new heart. Your old heart has no good soil within it. Because of apathy and sin, it has cultivated only rocks and weeds that choke God's Word from your life. Watch out—apathy kills!

> *Spiritual laziness leaves no other alternative but to live a reckless existence!*

Spiritual apathy has no built-in defense system; nothing "foreign" can be shielded off. Spiritual laziness leaves no other alternative but to live a reckless existence! Lazy people do not digest the Word; they do not have the ability to break it down. They are defenseless against the enemy's thrust into "unbridled sensuality" (Eph. 4:19). That is why we are appalled at what we see in this world—cloning of human beings, men changing their sex to become women, women becoming men—all kinds of degradation, because this world has become a prey.

The heart races to impurity because that is its nature. My pastor often told us, "If you take a hog out of the hog pen, put a white bow on it, get him all clean and sit him in a white living room on a white couch, the first time that hog sees slop, he is going to run out of that house and back to the slop, because that is his nature."

We try to dress people up in the church. We have incredible stained-glass windows and the most beautiful churches the world has ever seen. But the minute the body of Christ, the spiritually lazy people resting in the pews, sees the devil's slop—sexual impurities, lies and deceit—they run right back to it because that is still their nature.

Our loving heavenly Father has given us the solution to our spiritual laziness and apathy. God is saying to us:

I'll give you a new heart. I'll put a new spirit in you. I'll cut out your stone heart and replace it with a red-blooded, firm-muscled heart. Then you'll obey my statutes and be careful to obey my commands. You'll be my people! I'll be your God!

—Ezekiel 11:19–20, The Message

Our loving heavenly Father has given us the solution to our spiritual laziness and apathy.

MATTERS
SECTION
OF THE
FOUR
HEART

Devotions for Women

EXPOSING THE DECEPTION OF
THE OLD HEART

THIS DECEITFUL HEART

DOES NOT HAVE

WHAT IT TAKES TO BE

FAITHFUL TO ANYTHING—

GOD OR MAN.

BLESSED ARE THE PURE IN HEART

When God began dealing with me about my need for a new heart, this beatitude came alive in my spirit: "Blessed are the pure in heart, for they shall see God" (Matt. 5:8, NKJV). How could this happen? Why would God take me back to when I first learned about Him?

> *"I will not reveal My secrets to those whose hearts and motives are not pure."*

I remembered that I had always interpreted it to say, "Blessed are the pure in heart, for one day, when we die and go to heaven, we shall see God." The Lord began to say to me, "I desire that your spiritual eyes see Me now, but the only way that I can reveal My mysteries to you is according to My Word... the mysteries not yet revealed to man." In Jeremiah 33:3, God said, "Call to Me and I will answer you and show you great and mighty things, fenced in and hidden, which you do not know (do not distinguish and recognize, have knowledge of and understand)."

The Lord further said to me, "I will show you secrets that have not yet been revealed to man. I will not reveal My secrets to those whose hearts and motives are not pure." Then He added, "If you want to see Me in a way that you have never seen Me before, then I am compelling you to get a new heart—a pure heart."

I tried to respond by saying, "Well . . . I am struggling, and I see some things . . . I know that everything in my heart is not right. God, I just want You to fix it." God revealed to me that He had no desire to reconstruct and "fix" my old heart. His desire and purpose was to give me a new heart. Deep down, I knew that He was right.

I began to face what I call "the truth of all truth." Some of those actions repeated themselves over and over again, even after much time in prayer about them. I sought the Lord even more intently and said, "God, above everything . . ." I put my ministry, fame and television personality on the back burner. I said to God, "I do not care what comes and what goes. Most of all, I want to make sure that I am saved for real."

⟡

*You're blessed when you're at the end of your rope. With less
of you there is more of God and his rule.*
—MATTHEW 5:3, THE MESSAGE

⟡

God revealed to me that He had no desire
to reconstruct and "fix" my old heart. His
desire and purpose was to give me a new
heart.

DESIRE GOD—NOT JUST HIS BENEFITS

God began to say to me, "In this hour I am calling forth my prophets to purify themselves so that they will not prophesy through eyes of deception. Looking at this 'glorious' church and prophesying of her beauty, they have not been able to see on the inside of the church. She is full of lawlessness and iniquity and everything that is impure and unclean."

He told me, "I want you to begin to 'major' in what I am majoring in right now. It is a fact that I am taking My people along a certain route, and I am blessing them. I am allowing them to get the things that their hearts desire, because this will be the catalyst that I will use to prove to them that it was never Me they wanted. They wanted Me for things—they wanted Me for a car, they wanted Me for a house, they wanted Me for a job and for a new husband.

> *Many believers are like the Israelites who wandered away from Him.*

"When I give them everything that their heart desires, and when a newfound walk in Me does not come out of that, or a new heart, then I am showing them that they were never after a walk of righteousness when they came to Me." Then He showed me that many believers are like the Israelites who wandered away from Him. His response through Jeremiah to these wayfaring Israelites is His response to His church today:

> Then GOD said of these people: "Since they loved to
> wander this way and that, never giving a thought to
> where they were going, I will now have nothing
> more to do with them—except to note their guilt
> and punish their sins."
> —JEREMIAH 14:10, THE MESSAGE

In the holy place, where only priests could enter, the golden
altar rested in the center—the heart of the tabernacle. This is
where our hearts should be—because this is where true relationship with God is birthed. And like the tabernacle, it is the only
place that will usher us into His presence.

God is calling us today—as leaders—to get real and set the
pace for others. We must pursue the new heart, or we will not be
able to understand and obey what He is telling us to do.

> *Let my cry come right into your presence, GOD; provide me*
> *with the insight that comes only from your Word . . . And*
> *should I wander off like a lost sheep—seek me! I'll recog-*
> *nize the sound of your voice.*
> —PSALM 119:169, 176, THE MESSAGE

God is calling us today—as leaders—to get
real and set the pace for others.

The Weakness of the Old Heart

When pride invades our thoughts, we develop the tendency to always cover up. This builds counterfeit walls that must be whitewashed with the "appearance" of righteousness. God has started to reveal to me that covering up is not always the best way to help people. God has shown me that conducting our lives so as to look like "The Untouchables"—looking like we have it all together, like we are perfect—does not leave a straight path for others to follow.

Many believers are "taken out" and slaughtered in the battle of the Lord!

God explained to me, "I am trying to show you that when you get a new heart, you may be tempted from without, but there is no sin from within. That which is coming 'from without' will not find a match or an identification with anything that is 'within' you. You will be able to stand in times of testing. You will be able to stand against temptation. You will be able to stand against the wiles of Satan."

Then He said: "You have not fortified the walls of My people; you have not 'deposited' in them to the degree that their inner man has been strengthened against the onslaught of Satan." Because His prophets have not done this, today we watch as many believers are "taken out" and slaughtered in the battle of the Lord! Whitewashed walls are easily blown down by the enemy. They don't have the divine strength to stand.

The disciples learned how to submit by watching Jesus' example. He taught them, by example, how to be persecuted without warring back. He showed them how to suffer for righteousness' sake. He showed them how to go to the cross and die for the sins of the world. He demonstrated how to sacrifice and lay down their lives for a brother. He showed them how to "stand in the gap" for someone that needed God.

Jesus lived a pattern. As a result, when Peter was persecuted, he knew how to die. Paul knew how to die. The disciples and early followers of Jesus had all been taught how to die. They understood the pattern and knew how to stand in the battle of the Lord.

God is strong, and he wants you strong. So take everything the Master has set out for you, well-made weapons of the best materials. And put them to use so you will be able to stand up to everything the Devil throws your way.
—EPHESIANS 6:10–11, THE MESSAGE

It was necessary for the disciples to learn how to follow the steps of Jesus, just as it had been necessary for Jesus to learn how to follow the steps of His Father.

CLINGING TO FALSE HOPES

The prophets who prophesied false hopes to the people caused men to believe that the "peace" about which they were prophesying was possible. They gave the impression that God was "understanding" of the spiritual lethargy present among His people.

Just as in the days of Ezekiel, people everywhere are trusting in the voice of the prophet who comes in God's stead. They are looking for a confirmation of what the prophet has spoken. But in reality, what the prophet has spoken is not what God is saying. Many people have become gripped by false hope, which will bring them into despair and land them in a final state of hopelessness. When hopelessness penetrates their trust in God, they will fall by the wayside.

> *Many people have become gripped by false hope, which will bring them into despair and land them in a final state of hopelessness.*

The Word of the Lord warned the false prophets in Ezekiel about giving false hopes to His people:

I'm dead set against prophets who substitute illusions for visions and use sermons to tell lies . . . The fact is that they've lied to my people. They've said, "No problem; everything's just fine," when things are not at all fine. When people build a wall, they're right

behind them slapping on whitewash. Tell those who
are slapping on the whitewash, "When a torrent of
rain comes and the hailstones crash down and the
hurricane sweeps in and the wall collapses, what's
the good of the whitewash that you slapped on so liberally, making it look so good?"
—EZEKIEL 13:8–12, THE MESSAGE

As men and women of God . . . as God's spokesmen in this dark
world, we must be certain that we have not prophesied false hope to
a spiritually lethargic people. False prophets shower people with
compliments, which builds a flimsy wall that collapses when trouble
comes. God speaks to those who "have an ear" for true revelation
that builds the inner man. It instructs, reproves, corrects, disciplines
and trains the new heart in righteousness. (See 2 Timothy 3:16.)

*GOD judges persons differently than humans do. Men and
women look at the face; GOD looks into the heart.*
—1 SAMUEL 16:7, THE MESSAGE

God is warning against taking on the cloak
of the outward appearance. When the
enemy comes in and when the storms of
life are blowing, many fall by the wayside.

ENSLAVED BY DECEPTION

We are living in the final hour, and the glamour of the world is causing us to be tricked by the enemy. The "outer cloak" is deceiving us. The Word of the Lord is constantly ringing in my spirit that we have the "form of godliness," but we are "denying the power thereof" (2 Tim. 3:5, KJV). We have everything that it takes to make up the "image" of God, but the real power is being able to say *yes* to God and *no* to the devil.

> *The "outer cloak" is deceiving us.*

This is my assignment—not to encourage people in doing wrong, but to show God's people where their lives are wrong. To reveal the power of God's Word, which will enable the people to cast off the deception of the outer cloak, the "form of godliness."

We cannot allow ourselves to be enslaved to deception, especially while we are doing God's work! We must serve God from a new heart, one that only He can give and that we must maintain. He is charging us to turn it around, to set our faces like "flint" toward His divine purpose in this final hour. Blood is required when you see danger and fail to warn the wicked. (See Ezekiel 3:18.)

God is looking over your shoulder...so proclaim the Message with intensity; keep on your watch. Challenge, warn, and urge your people. Don't ever quit. Just keep it simple...Keep your eye on what you're doing...do a thorough job as God's servant.

—2 TIMOTHY 4:1–2, 5, THE MESSAGE

He is charging us to turn it around, to set our faces like "flint" toward His divine purpose in this final hour.

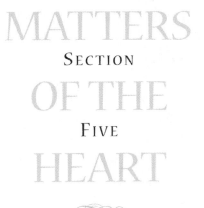

MATTERS OF THE HEART

SECTION FIVE

Devotions for Women

UNDERSTANDING THE OLD HEART

WE ARE BLINDED BY

OUR OWN DECEPTION.

WE ARE BLINDED BY

THE "OLD HEART."

ABUSING GOD'S GRACE

Many times believers abuse the fact that there is a "grace factor" in our walk with God. We assume a comfortable position where we do not have to change certain behaviors because we know that grace is there. Through our own spiritual laziness, we are using the liberty of Christ as an occasion for the flesh.

Through our own spiritual laziness, we are using the liberty of Christ as an occasion for the flesh.

Paul spoke to this issue in the sixth chapter of Romans by saying: "So what do we do? Keep on sinning so God can keep on forgiving? I should hope not! If we've left the country where sin is sovereign, how can we still live in our old house there? Or didn't you realize we packed up and left there for good?" (Rom. 6:1–2, THE MESSAGE).

After God birthed this truth into my spirit, I began recognizing personality traits manifesting from within me that were evidence of the old heart. Each time this happened, I would simply say, "Lord, forgive me." But after a period of time, they would resurface—sometimes on a daily basis!

I know that God was giving me opportunities to allow my mind to be transformed. But, like many other people, rather than spending quality time to find out why these shortcomings kept surfacing and trying to understand why I kept failing in those areas, for the sake of comfort I attached those things to myself and said, "This is just the way I am. God understands the way I am." I had made myself comfortable, and I settled into this lethargic frame of mind.

When you fall into this trap, it extends to your inner circle and to your immediate surroundings. Then the deception worsens. Rather than you having to adjust and change some things about your personality and character, your friends and associates begin to accept that behavior as just being "you" because it has become such a part of you. As a result, you stay the way you are.

The Lord began to make me understand that He was not requiring me to *adjust* these shortcomings for acceptance sake— *He was requiring me to change.*

<hr />

That means you must not give sin a vote in the way you con- duct your lives. Don't give it the time of day. Don't even run little errands that are connected with that old way of life. Throw yourselves wholeheartedly and full-time—remem- ber, you've been raised from the dead!—into God's way of doing things.
—ROMANS 6:12–13, THE MESSAGE

<hr />

Don't abuse God's grace by ignoring it so you can stay in your spiritual comfort zone. Get up, get out and get moving with God.

DECEIVED BY OUR OWN "PERFECTION"

The first thing God had to break was my deception about myself, because "the heart is hopelessly dark and deceitful" (Jer. 17:9, THE MESSAGE). My own heart was deceiving me. That got me! After being raised in the church and being saved, I constantly "fell away," doing things that were outside God's will. I came to this realization—your heart can be deceived without your knowing it, because you live for God from the "religious factor."

> *There is much more to following Him than stumbling and blundering around with the crowd.*

What do I mean by a religious factor? It's when we compare our righteousness to the righteousness of other people rather than to God's. When you compare yourself with someone else, your heart deceives you into thinking, *I am not all that bad. Look at how bad So-and-so is.* Or you could compare yourself with someone and think, *Well, he and I, or she and I, are a lot alike, so I am not all that bad.*

You begin to identify with the behavior of others, attempting to mimic "the going personality" in Christendom at the time. Everybody does the same thing—that which is familiar and acceptable. We are all stuck in a bucket like a bunch of crabs, saying, "This is the 'Christian' way, and everybody is like this." Everyone settles in and gets comfortable with that particular lifestyle until the Lord reveals to someone that there is more. There is much more to following Him than stumbling and blundering around with the crowd.

If you ask God for the new heart, you can begin to pursue the perfection of God and walk out what you believe to the extent that your heart becomes "perfected" in Him.

When this happens, you will stop comparing yourself to others. You will allow God to evaluate you properly. He can inspect your heart and give you the right grade. If He gives your heart an F, then you know it is failing, as mine was. But God will give you a new heart!

We've sinned and kept at it so long! Is there any hope for us? . . . We're all sin-infected, sin-contaminated. Our best efforts are grease-stained rags.
—ISAIAH 64:5–6, THE MESSAGE

If you ask God for the new heart, you can begin to pursue the perfection of God and walk out what you believe to the extent that your heart becomes "perfected" in Him.

FALLING AWAY STEP BY STEP

How do you know when you need a new heart? How do you know the difference between making a mistake and falling away from your first love? Ephesians 4 gives us a step-by-step process to recognize when you have fallen away from your first love and need a new heart.

> *Our hearts have become hardened and insensitive to what is right before God.*

A "futile" mind is incapable of producing any result (v. 17). It is ineffective, useless and unsuccessful. It does not yield anything that is fruitful or beneficial.

Your moral understanding is darkened (v. 18). When you start doing ungodly things and yet try to justify why you are doing it, your moral understanding is darkened, and your reasoning is beclouded.

You explain away your actions according to worldly knowledge and carnal information (v. 18). We are living in a brain world, which moves according to knowledge, not according to the new heart. As a result, we try to cover our actions by "explaining them away" according to worldly knowledge and carnal information.

You persistently do things your own way (v. 18). We

have become willfully blinded, not incapable of seeing. That is why this verse says the blindness is "deep-seated." We have been doing something a certain way for so many years we believe that we are walking in God's ways when in fact we are in error. Our hearts have become hardened and insensitive to what is right before God.

You indulge in every impurity that comes your way (v. 19). You may have learned the vocabulary of Scripture, but you have not spiritually comprehended the purpose and reason why Christ died. Since you have not learned Christ (the Living Word), you indulge in every impurity that comes your way. Righteousness, to you, is simply words on paper—not flesh and blood. As a result, you live to feed your flesh. Do you see a negative pattern forming in your life? If so, you need a new heart.

Don't grieve God. Don't break his heart. His Holy Spirit, moving and breathing in you, is the most intimate part of your life, making you fit for himself. Don't take such a gift for granted.

—EPHESIANS 4:30, THE MESSAGE

Do you see a negative pattern forming in your life? If so, you need a new heart.

73

THE DECEPTION OF "CONTROL"

Have you ever been in a situation where you said to yourself, "I will never do this," or "I will never do that"? I cannot tell you how many times I said that I would never do something, and then ended up doing just that. This is because the old heart is on a timetable, to the degree that when it is allowed to remain within you, it becomes stronger by being fed the worldly knowledge from the brain.

Transformation takes place when our minds are brought to the understanding that we need God.

It starts small, with the things that you "think" you can control—which becomes the next deception of Satan. He allows you to think that you are in control of this "old heart." He allows you to think, *I have it under control. I only drank one drink.* Or, *I only smoked one cigarette.* He knows that if you keep going—keep letting that heart go unchallenged, unchanged and unconverted—everything in that old heart (that he has birthed into the world) will be made manifest in your life.

This heart will never lead you to life, because it does not have life in it. It will never lead you to eternal truth, because this heart does not have the ability to house the Word of the Lord. Transformation can only take place when our minds are brought to the understanding that we need God.

What a privilege and an honor it is when God calls us out of sin and gives us the opportunity to become acquainted with Him! This is the biggest miracle that can happen in your life, because—in the midst of having a mind that has been "conceived" in sin and "shaped" in iniquity, trained by the world and the enemy to the point that you have come into the world prepared to die an eternal death—God is still able to penetrate it.

For the Lord gives skillful and godly Wisdom; from His mouth come knowledge and understanding ... and the person of understanding will acquire skill and attain to sound counsel [so that he may be able to steer his course rightly].
—PROVERBS 2:6; 1:5

What a privilege and an honor it is when God calls us out of sin and gives us the opportunity to become acquainted with Him!

THE SPIRITUAL EMERGENCY ROOM

When we do not "renew" our minds, we can "fall away" into the old heart. I have learned that the brain never stops working. It never settles down, nor does it ever shut up. It is constantly receiving information at breakneck speed. The majority of the time, the heart cannot, and will not, keep up with the pace of the mind.

We may have living, functioning hearts that keep our physical bodies alive, but spiritually, without a heart transplant, we are dead.

I recently had to be taken to the emergency room because I did not understand this principle. You see, many times we are so busy moving and doing things that we do not consider our hearts. I didn't, and I started experiencing the symptoms. I ended up in the emergency room with chest pains. The doctors started talking to me about heart attacks. As they talked, they explained how defibrillators jump-start a heart that has stopped beating.

This incident reminded me of the church. There are so many Christians racing around with spiritual "heart problems" that we need to be resurrected when we get to church! The choir, the preacher and the praise and worship team have been our spiritual defibrillators—they get powered up and anointed with oil, and they send out an electrical charge into the congregation. They are trying to jump-start hearts that have literally stopped beating. The treatment keeps you going for a couple of days, but that heart is still "mortally sick" (Jer. 17:9). It needs to be replaced.

In the natural realm, when someone has a heart attack, there are signs, sounds and different things that the diseased heart allows to happen in the physical body. There is pain that goes down the arm and down the legs because the arteries are having a hard time pumping blood to and from the heart.

The Bible says that we were "dead in trespasses and sins" (Eph. 2:1, KJV). We need to take a good, hard look at the state of our spiritual hearts. Are there any symptoms to alert us that our heart is diseased? Are there any habits we need to change to enhance the health of our spiritual hearts? We may have living, functioning, breathing hearts that keep our physical bodies alive, but spiritually, without a heart transplant, we are dead. Only a new heart will cause us to live forever.

≈≈≈

> *I the Lord search the mind, I try the heart, even to give to every man according to his ways, according to the fruit of his doings.*
> —JEREMIAH 17:10

≈≈≈

Only a new heart will cause us to live forever.

"Vital Signs" of Spiritual Trouble

We cannot turn on the news anymore without hearing about disaster. People are starving; cities are being flooded; fires cannot be put out; there are terrorist attacks. In other countries people are using their own bodies to blow up malls and shopping centers. Children are being raped, and the homeless are going unfed. God help us to discern the "signs" of worldwide heart failure.

If you do not wash your heart, the very thing that you once enjoyed with this old heart will ambush you.

The same types of things happened in the Bible when people ignored God and refused to learn His ways. Romans 6:23 says, "For the wages which sin pays is death."

This reminds me of King Uzziah. He prospered as long as he sought the Lord, and then he became strong *in his own mind*. When pride lifted him up, destruction soon followed. (See 2 Chronicles 26.) In a moment, he became a leper and lost his kingdom. Remember, whether you're a king or a servant, you will not be able to see God until the "brain" child dies.

We have knowledge about doing good, but we do not know how to do it. The know-how to "do good" requires a combination of a new heart and a transformed mind. The heart understands, and the mind knows. When both are in operation, the good in the heart flows to the mind and trains it with "know-how" to live according to God's Word. This renewed mind passes on the manifestation to the physical body.

According to His sovereign will, God has ordained that small things can overcome the mighty—because everything is in His hand. However, the problem is that our priorities are out of order. Many of us still have an old heart, so we cannot love God or fear Him unto obedience.

> It's the way you've lived that's brought all this on you. The bitter taste is from your evil life. That's what's piercing your heart.
>
> —JEREMIAH 4:18, THE MESSAGE

These distressing problems are our vital signs, letting us know that it is time to receive a new heart.

SYMPTOMS OF HEART FAILURE

God does not want us to be destroyed. He does not desire for us to be tormented by the ways of this world. Instead, He gives His people divine warnings to get their attention and to compel them to change their ways. That is why He is warning us right now. He is telling us, "It is time to receive a new heart."

> *The most powerful sign of your need for a new heart is these four golden words: "My heart is faint."*

Divine warnings are the advance symptoms of heart failure. Did you know that in today's medical industry it is virtually impossible to receive a new heart unless the old heart fails you? You cannot get a new heart until the old one breaks down—until it is starting to destroy your life. Then, and only then, will doctors recommend you for a heart transplant. Even in the natural realm, new hearts are in short supply.

Examine your heart right now. Ask yourself, "Is my heart destroying my life?" If so, you are a candidate for a heart transplant...but it does not stop there. You have to get up and go to the doctor in order to receive treatment. The doctor does not have a way of knowing that you need a heart transplant. You have to initiate the treatment, or the doctor cannot help you.

The most powerful sign of your need for a new heart is these four golden words: "My heart is faint." God's vital signs of breakdown will bring you to this place. This is God's heart—that you would understand and know that you need a new heart. He is waiting for you to say, "I cannot survive with this old heart. It has destroyed everything around me. It is destroying everything within me, and the number one thing that I cannot bear is the fact that I find no comfort in You, God. You are not my Comforter, so how can I survive without You?"

When that is the cry of your heart, God is telling you that you need a new heart.

Listen to the terms of this covenant and carry them out! I warned your ancestors when I delivered them from Egypt and I've kept up the warnings. I haven't quit warning them for a moment. I warned them from morning to night: "Obey me or else!" But they didn't obey. They paid no attention to me. They did whatever they wanted to do, whenever they wanted to do it, until I finally stepped in and ordered the punishments set out in the covenant, which, despite all my warnings, they had ignored.

—JEREMIAH 11:7–8, THE MESSAGE

This is God's heart—that you would understand and know that you need a new heart.

MATTERS
SECTION
OF THE
SIX
HEART

Devotions for Women

A SCIENTIFIC POINT OF VIEW

EVERYTHING THAT
GOD DOES HAS AN
EXPLANATION, SYMBOL
OR EXAMPLE IN
THE NATURAL REALM.

FEARFULLY AND WONDERFULLY MADE

When I started studying about the heart and brain, I was literally amazed—at times shocked into silence. More than this, I stood in awe of God, realizing how incredibly He has built us.

Allow me to give you a few "heart facts." The heart generally functions for seventy to eighty years without maintenance or replacement. During this time, it beats around one hundred thousand times a day, roughly forty million times a year—almost three billion beats in a lifetime. The heart pumps two gallons of blood per minute, adding up to more than one hundred gallons per hour, through a vascular system that is long enough to wrap around the earth two times—over sixty thousand miles. That powerful organ sits inside each person.[1]

When heart rhythms are in balance, like a mighty waterfall, it releases a balanced flow that resonates throughout our being.

The heart is the center of our being and allows us to function in harmony. It is like a nuclear power plant. It generates five thousand times more energy than the brain. Even more amazing, it has its own nervous system that is called the "brain of the heart." This "heart brain" has more than forty thousand nerve cells, the same number of cells contained in many of the brain's subcortical centers. Research has proven that the heart brain can and does act independently of the brain in your head![2]

The heart's power center directs and aligns many of our bodies' systems and helps them to function in harmony. And when heart rhythms are in balance, like a mighty waterfall, it releases a balanced flow that resonates throughout our being.

I pray that you will give God the glory and honor that He deserves. I pray that by learning these incredible truths, your love for Him will grow deeper. We are truly "fearfully and wonderfully made" (Ps. 139:14, KJV). David also said in this verse, "Wonderful are Your works, and that my inner self knows right well." Understanding God's works changed his soul! It can change yours.

I pray that, like me, you will read on and say to God, "I lay my life—everything that I am—down at Your feet." I pray that you will ask Him for a new heart.

Oh yes, you shaped me first inside, then out; you formed me in my mother's womb. I thank you, High God—you're breathtaking! Body and soul, I am marvelously made! I worship in adoration—what a creation!
—PSALM 139:13–14, THE MESSAGE

The heart is the center of our being and allows us to function in harmony.

HEART VISION

How can we have "heart vision"—how can we see from a heavenly perspective, according to the Word of God? There is a distinct difference between "knowing" and "understanding." The heart is the center of our understanding and can send waves of rational, considerate instruction to the brain. If the busy brain receives this instruction, it brings a balanced perspective, which can strengthen our conscience. However, the old heart does not have the spiritual power to override the brain's constant activity. This is why even our human conscience can be deceived.

> *The heart is the center of our understanding—where concepts and balanced intelligence are introduced to every part of us.*

In John 8, the scribes and Pharisees brought a woman to Jesus who had been caught in the act of adultery. The religious leaders reminded Him of the Law—she should be put to death (vv. 3–5). After listening to their argument, Jesus said to them, "He that is without sin among you, let him first cast a stone at her" (v. 7, KJV). The Word from Jesus' mouth penetrated their "old hearts" and revealed their hypocrisy—so they left with their old hearts intact.

Their old hearts could understand their own guilt, but they did not have the power to convert and save their souls! They had enough "conscience" to convict a woman.

It takes a pure, new heart to create a pure, undefiled conscience. Jesus turned to the woman in John 8 and gave her the solution: "'I am the light of the world: he that followeth me shall not walk in darkness, but shall have the light of life" (v. 12, KJV). In other words, He was saying, "The men who accused you were walking in the deception of their own darkened, earthly consciences. But I am able to give you a new heart that will fill your mind, and every part of you, with light—a balanced, complete, heavenly vision and understanding." That is powerful!

My son, attend to my words; consent and submit to my sayings. Let them not depart from your sight; keep them in the center of your heart. For they are life to those who find them, healing and health to all their flesh. Keep and guard your heart with all vigilance and above all that you guard, for out of it flow the springs of life.

—PROVERBS 4:20–23

"I am able to give you a new heart that will fill your mind, and every part of you, with light—a balanced, complete, heavenly vision and understanding."

BALANCE BETWEEN HEART AND MIND

The heart is universal; the brain is territorial. The brain begins to develop after the heart has already been formed—God created the heart to govern the brain. The heart is outside the brain and, technically, is not subject to brain processes. However, when we choose to ignore our heart's direction, the brain assumes control. It takes over, operating from a linear and logical perspective, always ready to defend its own interests. The brain has no understanding, so it is territorial—nothing foreign (spiritual) can enter without a fight.

It is a matter of the heart— the choice is yours.

The brain tries to pass on information to the heart, but the heart does not have to accept it. And this is where we encounter the mystery of the new heart. Logically, our old heart (by virtue of how God created it) should be able to override the brain. However, Adam and Eve perverted this ability when they followed their brains instead of their hearts (the enemy's great deception) in the Garden of Eden (Gen. 3). Now, in order to balance and control the mind, we must receive the new heart.

Jesus said that unless we become simple, like a child, we cannot enter His kingdom. We have to reject our logic and emotions, and with wide-open eyes, turn around and embrace the spiritual truth that flows from our new hearts.

Come, you children, listen to me; I will teach you to revere and worshipfully fear the Lord... The Lord is close to those who are of a broken heart and saves such as are crushed with sorrow for sin and are humbly and thoroughly penitent.
—PSALM 34:11, 18

The brain tries to pass on information to the heart, but the heart does not have to accept it.

DEVELOPING THE HEART AND MIND

When a child is conceived in the mother's womb, the first thing that develops is a heartbeat. After determining that a woman is pregnant, the heartbeat is the first thing the doctor goes after. He does not examine the mother, first looking for the eyes, nose, brain and nervous system. He listens for a heartbeat, and if there is a heartbeat, the child is alive.

It is imperative— especially during the first five years of your walk with God—that you spend time in the Word, worship and prayer in order to transform your mind.

As that baby begins to grow, by the time that child is six months old, the record of its experiences has escalated at an unbelievable rate. This is where the problem begins—the heart inside a six-month-old baby has already had six months' accumulation of memories in the world. That baby's brain, with its four different sections, is constantly being fed instant information from society. Already, more information is coming into the brain than the immature heart can handle. Because the brain is receiving more information than the heart can process, the brain "perceives" that it should govern that heart and body. This same struggle happens in the spiritual realm.

The next stage of a Christian's development is the formative years. Psychologists have proven that, without fail, by the time a child reaches five years of age, his or her heart and mind patterns are basically set for life. This same stage applies to our spiritual lives. It is imperative—especially during the first five years of your walk with God—that you spend time in the Word, worship and prayer in order to transform your mind.

When you are more mature, have learned your heart's rhythm and experienced what happens when you react to information that has been "spit out" by the brain—real or perceived—the results you have suffered teach you not to do that again. The mind needs to be retrained with the understanding that is built by the new heart—which is the heart of God. It must be retrained through the Word of God. Then the emotional and rational memory banks will be refilled with godly information from the Bible.

Don't lazily slip back into those old grooves of evil, doing just what you feel like doing. You didn't know any better then; you do now. As obedient children, let yourselves be pulled into a way of life shaped by God's life, a life energetic and blazing with holiness.

—1 PETER 1:13–14, THE MESSAGE

The mind needs to be retrained with the understanding that is built by the new heart—which is the heart of God.

THE NEW HEART AND A RENEWED MIND

The new heart and the renewed mind are a powerful combination. When understanding flows from the heart to the renewed mind, it identifies with what is already there and causes the body to receive the blessing. The mind is first "emotional," so the Word of God must enter the mind on a constant basis and create an emotional connection to the heart of God within you. Then, and only then, will your decisions be balanced by God's Word. Light and harmony will flood your entire being. With heart and brain unified (aligned), you will experience a natural flow, rhythm and peace within—no matter what is going on in the natural world.

The only thing that gives you control over the enemy is the synergy of the new heart and a renewed mind that is fully submitted to God and His will.

We cannot let the mind control us. We must ask for a new heart and then begin to obey the divine messages that God sends from within us. When we do, we will walk in divine authority because we will be in sync with the way God intended us to be. And when we are in sync with what God intended, the devil has to flee from us when we resist him (James 4:7).

When you have been born again, you may constantly look for and seek God in prayer for anointing and authority over the enemy because you do not understand that you already have the power to defeat him within you. The only thing that gives you control over the enemy is the synergy of the new heart and a renewed mind that is fully submitted to God and His will.

As your submit your mind to the will of God, which flows from your new heart, then this heart begins to rule and dominate your flesh and influence your surroundings. Since God resides in your new heart, and the character of God is already in it, you are automatically placed in a seat above Satan! You do not have to pray to get there. Your new heart transforms you to your rightful place. And, as you surrender your mind on a daily basis, it keeps you there.

God is telling us like never before—we need a new heart.

***

So be subject to God. Resist the devil [stand firm against him], and he will flee from you . . . When the righteous cry for help, the Lord hears, and delivers them out of all their distress and troubles.

—JAMES 4:7; PSALM 34:17

***

Since God resides in your new heart, and the character of God is already in it, you are automatically placed in a seat above Satan!

MATTERS

SECTION

OF THE

SEVEN

HEART

Devotions for Women

SPIRITUAL HEART SURGERY

THE NEW HEART

SETS US FREE,

DRESSES US FOR BATTLE

AND PUTS US RIGHT BACK

IN ACTIVE DUTY.

A Spiritual Heart Transplant

We have learned how the old heart is conceived and developed, and that it forms the basis of who we are. Now we will take a look at it from another angle. We all have a natural heart, but not many have new hearts that they have received from God. In the natural realm, when a surgeon says that a heart transplant is necessary, it is a matter of life and death.

God has already provided a Donor for all who desire to undergo this vital procedure. The heart that rested inside Jesus is available for transplant into your life.

This is the same in the spiritual realm. God has already said that the heart "is exceedingly perverse and corrupt and severely, mortally sick! Who can know it [perceive, understand, be acquainted with his own heart and mind]?" (Jer. 17:9). We desperately need a spiritual heart transplant!

God has already provided a Donor for all who desire to undergo this vital procedure. The heart that rested inside Jesus is available for transplant into your life. It is a heart of power. Jesus' heart came with an eternal assignment—and when we receive His heart, we receive our part of that mission. But just as the person who receives a transplanted natural heart must engage in a fight to keep his or her body from rejecting that transplanted heart, so too the enemy fights us tooth-and-nail to try to make us reject our new heart. He knows that the only way he can delay or cause us to abort our divine assignment is to cause us to reject our new heart. The new heart brings new warfare because the enemy wants to keep us bound and ineffective. The new heart sets us free, dresses us for battle and puts us right back into active duty.

Some spiritual POWs never overcome the trauma of war. Even after they have been rescued and brought back home, their minds torment them with reruns of what used to be. Though they have been set free, they are spiritually paralyzed. Through torment and deception, the enemy has disabled them. They do not even try to walk in their newfound freedom. They need a new heart—just like the generation of Israelites who died in the wilderness because they were afraid to obey God's voice (Num. 32:13).

A new heart will I give you and a new spirit will I put within you, and I will take away the stony heart out of your flesh and give you a heart of flesh. And I will put My Spirit within you and cause you to walk in My statutes, and you shall heed My ordinances and do them.
—EZEKIEL 36:26–27

The new heart sets us free, dresses us for battle and puts us right back into active duty.

THE SUPERNATURAL POWER OF
THE NEW HEART

When you receive a new heart, you can expect a battle. Your flesh, and the outside world, will not give up control without a fight. When God spoke to the Israelites, who because of the continual disobedience flowing out of their old hearts and unrenewed minds had been taken captive and scattered out of the Promised Land, He promised to gather His people and to give them back their land. But it wouldn't be without a fight! Along with their new heart would come the courage to take possession of their land and clean out all the impurities.

Every memory Jesus has of the Father, from before the foundation of the world, is inside you. His experiences of walking with power and authority on earth and casting Satan down are stored in your new heart.

When Jesus talked with His own followers about living the "Christ life" with their new hearts, He said that the world would hate them for following God. The good news is that Jesus overcame the world (John 16:33). He died to give us a healthy, new heart, and when that heart is transplanted inside us, we have part of Jesus—the One who died and rose again—in our innermost being!

If you trust and obey your new heart, Jesus will work inside you until you do consistently what is pleasing to God (Phil. 2:13).

If you obey the Lord, your new heart will lead you through this life and into eternity. It is actually your deposit of eternity, because Christ has already passed through death and ascended to heaven.

God has an appointed time and a purpose for you on the earth. The only way you will fulfill that purpose and assignment is to trust and obey Him.

What eye has not seen and ear has not heard and has not entered into the heart of man, [all that] God has prepared (made and keeps ready) for those who love Him [who hold Him in affectionate reverence, promptly obeying Him and gratefully recognizing the benefits He has bestowed]. Yet to us God has unveiled and revealed them by and through His Spirit, for the [Holy] Spirit searches diligently, exploring and examining everything, even sounding the profound and bottomless things of God [the divine counsels and things hidden and beyond man's scrutiny].

—1 CORINTHIANS 2:9–10

If you have a new heart, you have super-natural power!

THE POWER OF A HEART TRANSPLANT

*I*n your physical body, your most powerful organ will pull the others into its force of energy. It is the same in the spirit realm. Your new heart, being the heart of God, has infinitely more power than anything else does. Change will come if you allow it. Are you ready to change?

Your new heart, being the heart of God, has infinitely more power than anything else does. Change will come if you allow it.

Though powerful, the old heart has been over-programmed (by the brain) from birth. Its natural rhythm has been distorted, so it pulls everything into an out-of-sync pattern. It does not maintain a healthy balance. Organs are in place but not functioning the way they should. That is why we need a new heart. We need the Lord to help us put everything into balance.

Your new heart has been designed to clear out everything that is unbalanced and deceitful. This transplant moves you from one place to another place. It changes you, step by step, from one stage into another. God is moving you toward your new assignment. Things may feel strange at first, but if you will submit to God, He will do His "perfect work" in you (2 Tim. 3:16–17; James 1:4).

Since your new heart is no longer connected to your brain, it lives totally from the power of God! It receives its "messages" from the "information" that has been stored deep in His heart. Whatever is programmed in your new heart when God sets it into your chest cavity is the assignment that you will begin to carry out—and that's when you will fulfill your purpose. If you can't find your purpose, the revelation of God is not in your heart. The new heart always reveals new purpose.

Let the wicked forsake his way and the unrighteous man his thoughts; and let him return to the Lord, and He will have love, pity, and mercy for him, and to our God, for He will multiply to him His abundant pardon. For My thoughts are not your thoughts, neither are your ways My ways, says the Lord . . . For as the rain and snow come down from the heavens, and return not there again, but water the earth and make it bring forth and sprout, that it may give seed to the sower and bread to the eater, so shall My word be that goes forth out of My mouth: it shall not return to Me void [without producing any effect, useless], but it shall accomplish that which I please and purpose, and it shall prosper in the thing for which I sent it.

—ISAIAH 55:7–8, 10–11

Since your new heart is no longer connected to your brain, it lives totally from the power of God!

STANDING AGAINST THE OLD MIND

The new heart has come to assume its rightful place of authority, and the brain is painfully aware of this. Scientists have said that the brain fears the heart, and I believe this is especially so once it is severed from its nerve connection.[3] The old mind knows that Someone else is in control. The new assignment in that heart is going to be fulfilled—with or without the brain's help.

When we are no longer obeying the old mind, it is being put to death. A paradigm shift is occurring. While the old mind is being put to death (as the result of reading and obeying God's Word), the new heart is replacing the old actions and patterns in the brain. As you sow to the Spirit, it is taking back the ground that Satan once occupied.

While the old mind is being put to death (as the result of reading and obeying God's Word), the new heart is replacing the old actions and patterns in the brain.

The mind is used to speeding, racing and responding to the worldly way of doing things. In other words, if you walk up to me and slap me, then my brain says, "I have been trained by society to slap you back."

But the new heart says, "Turn the other cheek." It tells you, "If a person wants your coat, give him your cloak also." The new heart tells us to walk a mile for peace (Matt. 5:39–41).

When an enemy comes against you and wounds you, the old mind says, "I do not want to have anything to do with you."

But the Word that flows from the new heart says, "Love your enemies, bless them that curse you, do good to them that hate you, and pray for them which despitefully use you" (Matt. 5:44, KJV). So you enter into immediate warfare, because the Word of God is piercing that old mind and literally "canceling out" worldly thought patterns.

It happens so regularly that it's predictable. The moment I decide to do good, sin is there to trip me up. I truly delight in God's commands, but it's pretty obvious that not all of me joins in that delight. Parts of me covertly rebel, and just when I least expect it, they take charge.
—ROMANS 7:21–23, THE MESSAGE

Remember, the "old man" dies daily, but the "new man" is renewed day by day. As you sow to the Spirit, your new heart is taking back the ground that Satan once occupied.

THE BATTLE GOES ON

When you obey the new heart's rulership, the Word actually begins to renew the mind from without and from within. The brain is sandwiched. You have the Word inside you and are putting the Word into you (from outside) by reading the Bible—which travels through your eyes and goes directly to the brain! So the old heart pattern is literally being squeezed out. That is why the battle rages and you feel the conflict inside you. Your thought patterns have been "dug in" for years and years.

When the flesh determines it no longer enjoys the assignment it has received from the mind because the new heart is convicting it, real change can begin.

It is important to understand the process of receiving the new heart. It begins one day as you sit in a church service. Someone asks you if you want to be saved, and you go to the altar and receive the new heart. At that moment, everything changes, sending signals to the brain that it is going to die. The first explosion goes off in the mind, which hates being out of control. It loathes being disconnected.

Even as you kneel at the altar, deciding to follow Christ, thoughts begin to dart through your mind: *I cannot give this up. I am not ready to do this. I am afraid that So-and-so will not understand.* This is your first battle in the war of your new heart. Your mind continues to perceive and conceive evil, but it does not have an old heart into which to plant the evil anymore. The new heart does not need the brain's input. It will not receive that earthly garbage. It is connected to eternity.

So the mind keeps throwing out its "alarm signals" to the flesh, for the body to obey its instructions and carry out the ungodly actions. The new heart responds by sending a wave of conviction, and the battle goes on. Soon the flesh determines that it no longer enjoys the assignment it has received from the mind because the new heart is convicting it. And that is when real change can begin.

At this point, the mind becomes outnumbered. It is sandwiched by the heart, which refused to obey, and the flesh, which is convicted about doing evil. The brain no longer has an accomplice to help carry out its wicked schemes! But the heart is embracing a partner to show forth the "good fruits" of repentance and holiness.

Be good to your servant, GOD; be as good as your Word. Train me in good common sense; I'm thoroughly committed to living your way. Before I learned to answer you, I wandered all over the place, but now I'm in step with your Word. You are good, and the source of good; train me in your goodness.
—PSALM 119:66–68, THE MESSAGE

The new heart is connected to eternity.

DON'T QUENCH THE SPIRIT

Your new heart is a powerful, yet gentle ruler. If you submit to its promptings in spite of your brain's resistance, the heart will send a message back to the brain that says, "I am not going to do it that way. I am not going to answer that way." As you submit to God, these messages will become so powerful that the body will divorce the brain waves and begin to line up with your new heart. This is not just a spiritual truth; it is a physical fact.

> *God continues to purge the "detestable things" in our flesh as we read and obey His Word.*

On the other hand, if the heart sends a clear, intuitive signal with a feeling that says, "Don't do this," the head may vigorously resist, demanding to know "Why? How? When?" so persistently that the heart's signal is cut off.[4] In Christendom, we call this "quenching the Spirit." This can also explain why it can be so difficult at times to pray or enter into true, heartfelt worship. First Thessalonians 5:19 says, "Do not quench (suppress or subdue) the [Holy] Spirit."

God continues to purge the "detestable things" in our flesh as we read and obey His Word. Everything "hidden" begins to be exposed and discarded as the Word digs up each impure thought and motive. Your battle will be to submit to the Spirit's direction, and this can be an awesome fight. If you do not submit to your new heart, ultimately you will be stripped by the enemy and thrown into a cold, dark place. Your new heart will bring you to a valley of decision as you go through the process of purification.

For example, if you read the scripture (outside information coming into your mind) that says, "Love thy neighbor as thyself," and your new heart (information from the heart of Christ) is already programmed to love your neighbor, when the evil thought arises to say, "Hate your neighbor," it will be ineffective. The message coming in that says, "Love thy neighbor," combines with the new heart desire to love already inside you and attacks that evil thought from both sides, squeezing it out.

When you submit to God, you can resist the devil, your mind and the evil influences of this world.

May God himself, the God who makes everything holy and whole, make you holy and whole, put you together—spirit, soul, and body—and keep you fit for the coming of our Master, Jesus Christ. The One who called you is completely dependable. If he said it, he'll do it!

—1 THESSALONIANS 5:23–24, THE MESSAGE

Your new heart is a powerful, yet gentle ruler.

"Spiritual Guppies"

It is God who determines how well we are progressing on our transformation into the Christ-life after we receive our new hearts. When we surrender our hearts to God and say, "No more!" to the struggle within, He will do battle on our behalf. He has already prepared a host of angels to fight for us. He has also prepared the Holy Spirit to stretch out the "measuring rod," so that this time when we come to Him, our hearts will be constructed properly.

We can submit to God's rebuilding process, or we can go back to the pit. The choice is ours.

God searches our hearts. He knows when our words come from the abundance of righteousness that He has stored within us. And these words—not the empty confessions from the brain—will yield eternal results, and our Father will be pleased.

He is faithful to tell us when we are doing well, not through somebody else's words and standards, but by speaking directly to our new heart, saying, "Well done, good and faithful servant" (Matt. 25:23, KJV). God's voice is the only one that really counts.

We can compliment each other, compare ourselves against one another and say many things—but we must realize that many who encourage us are still "guppies" in the Spirit. They are not "big fish" to God. They just seem to be because they are stroking our flesh. According to God's measuring line, they are not where they need to be. The danger of comparison surfaces again! In the ocean, a guppy would be so tiny that it would say to a goldfish, "Oh, you are such a big, beautiful, bright fish!" A shark, on the other hand, would see it differently.

Let us not think of ourselves "more highly" than we ought to think (Rom. 12:3). We are utterly dependent upon God and the new heart that He puts within us. If we fail to trust and obey Him as He begins to purify our earthly temples, we can be taken prisoner again by the enemy. We can submit to God's rebuilding process, or we can go back to the pit. The choice is ours. We need to embrace the new heart.

Now when he [the angel] had finished measuring the inner temple area, he brought me forth toward the gate which faces east and measured it [the outer area] round about . . . He measured it on the four sides; it had a wall round about the length five hundred reeds and the breadth five hundred, to make a separation between that which was holy [the temple proper] and that which was common [the outer area].

—EZEKIEL 42:15, 20

 God searches our hearts, and His voice is the only one that really counts.

SECTION

EIGHT

MATTERS OF THE HEART

Devotions for Women

UNDERSTANDING OUR NEW HEART

YOUR NEW HEART

HAS THE

UNDENIABLE ABILITY

TO WALK IN

THE STATUTES OF GOD.

THE MIND OF CHRIST

The new heart is an amazing mystery, and we must walk in the Spirit to understand its depths. We hold the feelings and purposes of God within us! That is awesome. Even more, our new heart leads us into the counsel of God as we submit to its direction. Yes, our new heart has a brain, and that brain is the mind of Christ.

> *Our new heart has a brain, and that brain is the mind of Christ.*

The old heart can function independently of the brain. The new heart also has this ability, but even more so—because it is supernatural. The old (natural) "nerve" connection has been severed, so this heart is able to rule your old brain because it was not with your original body at conception. It was never oversaturated with information by your old brain, so it has the power to take authority. This heart has not been naturally conditioned to bow to your mind through years of familiarity. Your new heart has the undeniable ability to walk in the statutes of God.

When you say, "I have been born again in Christ Jesus," the first thing that begins to function and rule in that space is the heart. When you have been converted for real, you receive a new heart, and that heart takes you back to the beginning—to when you were a fetus—because your new heart beats without being connected to the brain, just like in the unborn child.

After your "new birth"—your true conversion into the kingdom of God—the brain of your new heart takes over and controls what you do, guiding you into the ways of the Spirit and into obedience to the Father.

Jesus answered, I assure you, most solemnly I tell you, unless a man is born of water and [even] the Spirit, he cannot [ever] enter the kingdom of God. What is born of [from] the flesh is flesh [of the physical is physical]; and what is born of the Spirit is spirit . . . The wind blows (breathes) where it wills; and though you hear its sound, yet you neither know where it comes from nor where it is going. So it is with everyone who is born of the Spirit.
—JOHN 3:5–6, 8

After your "new birth"—your true conversion into the kingdom of God—the brain of your new heart takes over and controls what you do.

WAVES OF LIFE

Through its beating patterns, the heart sends pressure waves that move through our arteries to create our pulse rhythms. Heartbeats also influence brainwave activity and provide oxygen, nutrients and electrical energy to every organ and gland in our bodies.

Researchers have documented that when a pulse of blood gets up to the brain, it changes the brain's electrical activity. It alters the flow of that brain's process! Your new heart is also able to send "waves" of life, quickening your brain and the rest of your being to the ways of God.

> *Your new heart is also able to send "waves" of life, quickening your brain and the rest of your being to the ways of God.*

Of the trillions of cells in the human body, heart cells are the only ones that can pulsate. With every pulsation, "intelligent communication" takes place. According to cardio-energetics (a newer field of science), our heart mediates our thoughts, feelings, fears and dreams. It also keeps our bodies in chemical balance. Research has also revealed that the heart has a powerful impact outside the body as well. For example, when nurses played a recorded heartbeat in a hospital nursery, the crying was reduced by almost 55 percent. The beats become their rhythm—an emotional "life support" system.[5]

Unlike the brain, or any other organ in the body, our hearts can be felt, heard and sensed by us. Not only does our heart affect every cell in our bodies, but also its electromagnetic field has been measured to radiate outside the body, even up to ten feet away.[6] Any way you look at it, the heart is magnetic.

In the same way, your new spiritual heart influences the rest of you to follow the ways of God. It balances your urges and desires, as well as influences those around you, acting as a magnet to draw others to the Lord.

For you who welcome him [God], in whom he dwells—even though you still experience all the limitations of sin—you yourself experience life on God's terms. It stands to reason, doesn't it, that if the alive-and-present God who raised Jesus from the dead moves into your life, he'll do the same thing in you that he did in Jesus, bringing you alive to himself? When God lives and breathes in you (and he does, as surely as he did in Jesus), you are delivered from that dead life. With his Spirit living in you, your body will be as alive as Christ's!
—ROMANS 8:11–13, THE MESSAGE

The new heart balances your urges and desires, as well as influences those around you, acting as a magnet to draw others to the Lord.

Don't Be a Fish Out of Water!

God desires that we dedicate ourselves fully to Him, trusting in and obeying His instructions. As we do this, our new hearts are strengthened, and an atmosphere of righteousness, worship and purification is created that reminds your heart of its heavenly home.

Your new heart comes from a purified place, so in order for it to be strong enough to stay in a willing position, you have to keep it in this type of atmosphere.

Your new heart comes from the Spirit realm, so you have to keep it in the atmosphere of the Spirit in order for it to exist.

When a baby is delivered out of its mother's womb, the nurses wrap the baby up and hand it to the mother, who holds her baby close to her heart. This makes the newborn feel warm and protected, just like when that baby lived in the womb.

If you take a fish out of the ocean, it can survive as long as you put it back in water within a short period of time. You cannot take a fish out of the ocean, its place of origin where it survives and thrives, bring it home and lay it on your living room table. It will never live like that. If you take it from water where it is accustomed to living, you have to put it back into water in order for it to stay alive.

A baby fights to stay in the womb, and a fish will fight when you take it out of the water. It is the same with the new heart. It "hungers and thirsts" after righteousness—it will suffocate if you take it out of

God's presence. If you have a new heart, you should get to the point that you cannot get enough of God, church or God's people—because this heart lives and thrives in the atmosphere of worship.

This heart is bursting with the characteristics of Christ and longs for opportunities to express Christ through your actions. Because it hungers and thirsts for God, you must nourish it and feed it through your "Christ-life" living. Your new heart comes from the Spirit realm, so you have to keep it in the atmosphere of the Spirit in order for it to exist.

And those who belong to Christ Jesus (the Messiah) have crucified the flesh (the godless human nature) with its passions and appetites and desires. If we live by the [Holy] Spirit, let us also walk by the Spirit. [If by the Holy Spirit we have our life in God, let us go forward walking in line, our conduct controlled by the Spirit.]...make a decisive dedication of your bodies [presenting all your members and faculties] as a living sacrifice, holy (devoted, consecrated) and well pleasing to God, which is your reasonable (rational, intelligent) service and spiritual worship.
—GALATIANS 5:24–25; ROMANS 12:1

Because your new heart hungers and thirsts for God, you must nourish it and feed it through your "Christ-life" living.

THE RHYTHMS OF THE NEW HEART

There is another amazing thing about your heartbeat: It responds to music. So the heart produces rhythms, and it responds to the rhythm of song. It influences the autonomic (subconscious, automatic) functions of your body (like breathing, for example), and it gently begins to influence your behavior. How? Sometimes you will desire to do something that will please God, sometimes even before you have learned the scripture that tells you that is what you should do! (See 1 Thessalonians 4:1.)

Submit to the ways of God, and your new heart will thrive, bringing life to every other part of your being.

I have seen people who were converted who did not know the first thing about God before their conversion. They had not been raised in the church, yet they had an experience with God. After their conversion they started saying things like, "He told me to turn that movie off." "He told me to take those clothes off and not to wear that because it was too seductive." "He told me to take the earring out of my lip."

Sometimes I would ask, "You found that in the Scriptures?"

They would reply, "No, I have not read about it, but that is what God told me to do." They began to respond automatically to the new information flowing out of their new hearts.

When this occurs, it shows that you have been disconnected from your brain because you are no longer responding to its demands. You are obeying the gentle promptings of Almighty God! Because of that, you no longer follow the carnal, fleshly prompting of the flesh.

Do not be like a fish out of water. God does not want you to die! Submit to the ways of God, and your new heart will thrive, bringing life to every other part of your being. Let go and submit to the flow. Submit your ways unto the Lord, and your thoughts shall be established by the rhythms of your new heart.

Live freely, animated and motivated by God's Spirit. Then you won't feed the compulsions of selfishness. For there is a root of sinful self-interest in us that is at odds with a free spirit, just as the free spirit is incompatible with selfishness. These two ways of life are antithetical, so that you cannot live at times one way and at times another way according to how you feel on any given day. Why don't you choose to be led by the Spirit and so escape the erratic compulsions of a law-dominated existence?

—GALATIANS 5:16–18, THE MESSAGE

Just as the heart influences the autonomic functions of your body, the new heart will gently begin to influence your behavior.

THE OLD BRAIN AND THE NEW HEART

Our minds are determined to stay on top, be number one over our hearts and bodies (Gal. 5:26). So our minds have learned to keep gathering more and more information. The old mind tries to run the old heart into the ground as your brain attempts to keep up with the latest information, technology and everything else, just to stay competitive.

People can do evil things and think evil thoughts, and not be spiritually aware or pained by their actions, because they have cut off the intelligent language of their new heart.

When you become aware of the fact that you are jealous of people and competitive, it is time to make a change. Something is wrong if you are having these kinds of thoughts: *Do I preach better than this person? Who sings the best? Whose church is larger?* Such thoughts are the workings of your mind. They do not flow from the heart of God.

An interesting fact about the brain is that it has no feeling. If we apply this spiritually, we can discover why people can do evil things and think evil thoughts and not be spiritually aware or pained by their actions. They have cut off the intelligent language of their new heart.

The brain has so much information coming into it that it overloads and paralyzes the old heart. The old heart could not compete against it. This is one of the main reasons why your new heart has to be disconnected from the mind. Your new heart has come loaded with divine information that has not yet been revealed to man! So it always tells that old brain, "I know stuff that you do not know. I know things that your intellect could never comprehend! The only way you will ever be able to understand is if God reveals it to you!"

For whoever has [spiritual knowledge], to him will more be given and he will be furnished richly so that he will have abundance; but from him who has not, even what he has will be taken away . . . For this nation's heart has grown gross (fat and dull), and their ears heavy and difficult of hearing, and their eyes they have tightly closed, lest they see and perceive with their eyes, and hear and comprehend the sense with their ears, and grasp and understand with their heart, and turn and I should heal them.
—MATTHEW 13:12, 15

Your new heart has come loaded with divine information that has not yet been revealed to man!

THERE IS LIFE IN THE BLOOD

There is another, even more amazing thing about the new heart, old mind disconnection. Since the arteries, which transport the blood, are no longer connected by nerve endings to the old heart, they establish the connection to our new hearts. Praise God! Only by the blood can the heart rule the mind. The blood is how the new heart stays purified, because it is continuously cycled through the heart on its way to the rest of the body. The blood of Jesus can literally "wash away your sin," making you "white as snow" (pure) in His sight!

The spiritual DNA in our new blood makes us sons and daughters of God, causing us to look more like Him as we obey our new heart.

There is life in the blood! So when Jesus said, "You are cleansed and pruned already, because of the word which I have given you," He was revealing a spiritual process (John 15:3). The Word enters the mind and cleanses it; then the blood flows through and gives it life. The Word of God is alive because Jesus shed His blood and transformed typed pages into a living reality! His blood brings the Word alive. It makes the gospel work.

Even more than this, just as a heart transplant patient must receive life-giving blood transfusions as part of the transplant process, when you receive a new heart, you have also received new blood—Christ's blood!

This new blood identifies you with the Father and sets the atmosphere for the new heart. Let me illustrate. When people see my parents, it's obvious that I came from them. My outer appearance and my inner man reflect who they are. It is the same with the Lord. The spiritual DNA in our new blood is eternally new. It makes us "sons" and "daughters" of God, causing us to look more like Him as we obey our new heart. And believe me, a DNA test always reveals who the real father is!

Because of the sacrifice of the Messiah, his blood poured out on the altar of the Cross, we're a free people—free of penalties and punishments chalked up by all our misdeeds. And not just barely free, either. Abundantly free!
—Ephesians 1:7–8, The Message

The Word enters the mind and cleanses it; then the blood flows through and gives it life.

MATTERS
SECTION
OF THE
NINE
HEART

Devotions for Women

RENEWING THE MIND

ACCORDING TO MEDICINE,

THE HEART TRANSPLANT

IS IMMEDIATE, BUT THE

MIND TRANSFORMATION

IS PROGRESSIVE.

FOUR STAGES OF MIND TRANSFORMATION

When God gives you a new heart, it is the deposit, or assurance, from God that He is also going to make your mind new. The old (natural) brain is formed, step by step, into four different sections. Although you get a whole new heart at once, the mind must be transformed in stages and in levels. Going back to conception, the heart forms and beats before the brain is created. Then it grows from the bottom up, starting with the medulla, amygdala, cerebral cortex and finally the frontal lobes. According to medicine, the heart transplant is immediate, but the mind transformation is progressive.

For Christians, our daily battleground is the progressive state of renewing our minds.

The *medulla oblongata* establishes the link between the automatic functions of the heart, mind and body. Then the *amygdala* develops, which stores emotional memories and forms the basis of your perceptions. Out of the amygdala, the *logic centers* form, beginning with the cerebral cortex, where complex thought patterns like planning, strategizing, reflection, inspiration and imagination emerge. Lastly, the *frontal lobes* develop, allowing you to make decisions based on emotional and logical input. This section feeds back into the amygdala, telling it how to react or respond from the emotional memories.[7]

For Christians, our daily battleground is the progressive state of renewing our minds. As you submit to God through your new heart, He balances your entire being. Your body starts to pulse with the new rhythms from your new heart, blood pressure waves hit your brain, and the old mind begins to respond to the new flow of your heart. And although the immediate effect may be subtle, you discover that you no longer think the same way anymore. Subtly, but consistently, the way you think and the way you do things change.

Each stage of your mind's development must be renewed. The Word must "pierce" each part of the mind, transforming thought and emotion on the subconscious and conscious levels.

The plans of the mind and orderly thinking belong to man, but from the Lord comes the [wise] answer of the tongue. All the ways of a man are pure in his own eyes, but the Lord weighs the spirits (the thoughts and intents of the heart). Roll your works upon the Lord [commit and trust them wholly to Him; He will cause your thoughts to become agreeable to His will, and] so shall your plans be established and succeed.

—PROVERBS 16:1–3

As you submit to God through your new heart, He balances your entire being.

BETA: BRING GOD INTO
YOUR PROBLEM SOLVING

Just as there are four sections of the brain, there are four levels of consciousness called *brain waves*, or electrical currents that cycle through it. We know them as *Beta*, *Alpha*, *Theta* and *Delta*. They are measured by the power of the impulse, or frequency, as well as speed, which determines the category. Beta cycles through your brain eighteen to thirty times per second; Alpha is next at eight to twelve cycles, followed by Theta at four to seven cycles, and finally to Delta waves at less than six cycles per second. The faster the cycles, the higher your level of consciousness will be.[8]

> *Beta thoughts wear and tear on your heart if you remain on this level too long.*

Most people function on the Beta level while they are awake. This level is fast, but not the most efficient. The logic and problem solving of the frontal lobes and cerebral cortex are easiest in Beta; however, your thoughts often "collide" on this level. Researchers say that you cannot stop or slow Beta waves down long enough to focus on just one thought, causing you to miss important details. This is how the old mind deceives you. Logic and decision making, which require crystal-clear thinking, cannot be clear and focused when your heart and mind are out of balance.

Americans live in an instant society, so Beta thinking is very welcome here. We want things to happen fast, so we take things into our own hands. *God is not pleased.* Beta thoughts wear and tear on your heart (and your entire body) if you remain on this level too long. Yet the "ruling" brain loves Beta; it will keep you from slowing down and listening to your heart whenever it can. Like stress, Beta thinking can be a silent killer. Before you realize it, your thought patterns are in overdrive, and breakdown is imminent.

Lean on, trust in, and be confident in the Lord with all your heart and mind and do not rely on your own insight or understanding. In all your ways know, recognize, and acknowledge Him, and He will direct and make straight and plain your paths. Be not wise in your own eyes; reverently fear and worship the Lord and turn [entirely] away from evil. It shall be health to your nerves and sinews, and marrow and moistening to your bones.
—PROVERBS 3:5–8

Logic and decision making, which require crystal-clear thinking, cannot be clear and focused when your heart and mind are out of balance.

ALPHA: BE STILL AND KNOW THAT GOD IS IN CONTROL

Alpha bridges your conscious and subconscious minds. It has been called the most productive cycle, and it was the first that people learned to identify and control. Alpha is an alert, daydreaming state, a relaxed, detached awareness that reflects a receptive mind. Alpha seems to function primarily between the cerebral cortex and the amygdala. If Alpha is lost, the link to your subconscious mind is broken. You will not be able to remember details about your dreams or visions from God. Alpha is the link between "knowing" and "doing."

> *The Alpha state is where you have chosen to "be still" and know that God is in control.*

The Alpha state is where you have chosen to "be still" and know that God is in control (Ps. 46:10). It is the *meditative* state, where you are aware of your surroundings, but more tuned into your inner consciousness. Problem solving becomes easier, and your intuitions run deeper. You catch the thoughts that are missed in Beta.

Keep your mouth shut, and let your heart do the talking.
—PSALM 4:4, THE MESSAGE

Alpha is the link between "knowing" and "doing."

THETA: DON'T RUN AHEAD OF GOD

Theta is the next level, occurring while you are in a light sleep. Theta waves are slower than Alpha waves, but more intense, usually indicating emotional stimulation. They are linked with child-like thoughts and insecurities (children up to the age of puberty have high readings of Theta waves).[9] Theta waves seem to operate hand in hand with amygdala thinking, and they can also tap into deeper thought patterns. Flash insights come from the Theta realm. For example, have you ever thought, *Something is not right here . . . I do not know what it is, but something is wrong?*

So many times when something goes wrong, we think back on the incident and say, "I had a gut feeling!" In reality, our heart was forewarning us of danger.

Sometimes Theta brain waves relate to those *gut feelings* we all have from time to time. Have you ever thought, *Do not go that way*, but you went anyway? Then something happened that could have been avoided. Most likely, your new heart was connecting with Theta brain waves. So many times when something goes wrong, we think back on the incident and say, "I had a gut feeling!" In reality, our heart was forewarning us of danger—already having perceived what was going to happen—but we were not in the right state of consciousness to receive the full revelation.

We cannot speed around in Beta thinking and expect to have new heart insight. Many have been hurt, bruised and offended because their minds—*not* their hearts—were leading them.

Many plans are in a man's mind, but only that which is of the Lord will stand!

> *When the Friend comes, the Spirit of the Truth, he will take*
> *you by the hand and guide you into all the truth there is.*
> —JOHN 16:13, THE MESSAGE

Many have been hurt, bruised and offended because their minds—not their hearts— were leading them.

DELTA: ALL THINGS ARE POSSIBLE WITH GOD

Delta thinking is where "deep calleth unto deep"—the subconscious mind—where "all thy waves and thy billows are gone over me" (Ps. 42:7, KJV). This is the abyss, the deepest depth of your mind; you cannot measure, understand or control it. This is where God can change your temperament and behavior without you even knowing it! There is a saying: "A leopard can't change its spots." It can, and it will, if the Word of God is allowed to pierce on the Delta level.

Delta is where your mind can receive the "meat" of the Word as it pierces to the depths of your innermost being.

Delta is where your mind can receive the "meat" of the Word as it pierces to the depths of your innermost being—where Delta and Theta waves unite. Like a child, you embrace the truth and trust God with a deep, calm awareness. David said, "Even at night my heart instructs me" (Ps. 16:7, NIV). On the Delta thought level, "all things are possible with God" (Mark 10:27). This deep, subconscious transformation flows up—through your emotions and logic—to illuminate your entire being. When the new heart is in complete control, electric impulses are *supernatural*—because the natural link has been cut. This mind is controlled by the power of God!

142

*As the hart pants and longs for the water brooks, so I pant
and long for You, O God. My inner self thirsts for God, for
the living God. When shall I come and behold the face of
God? . . . Yet the Lord will command His loving-kindness in
the daytime, and in the night His songs shall be with me, a
prayer to the God of my life.*

—PSALM 42:1–2, 8

This deep, subconscious transformation
flows up—through your emotions and
logic—to illuminate your entire being.

HEART AND HEAD EMOTIONS

Conscious thought begins and ends in your emotions. Emotions give meaning to facts generated by your logic—that is why our logical centers grow out of our emotions. The word *emotion* literally means "energy in motion." It is a strong feeling—like love, anger, joy or sorrow—that moves us. Basically, emotional energy is neutral. It is our logical thoughts and physical reactions that make our emotions either positive or negative.

People tend to think that emotions come from the heart. The truth is that both our mind and heart drive them.

Heart emotions reflect emotional maturity; they are balanced and offer solutions to problems rather than participating in them.

Head emotions are self-centered and defensive. They are moved by "what you can do for me." They want instant gratification. They are like conditional love, which says, "I'll love you, if you love me and meet my needs." Brain emotions will *drive* you to do things that are unwise or dangerous.

Heart emotions run deeper and are selfless. They express themselves without expecting anything in return. Heart emotions reflect emotional maturity; they are balanced and offer solutions to problems rather than participating in them. They are like *agape* love, which is the love God shows to us. God, who understands our weaknesses, sees the problems we bring upon ourselves and helps us find solutions, yet He does not become entangled in our problems. He loves us in spite of ourselves, drawing us into a deeper relationship and fellowship with Him, where heart emotions can begin to renew the mind.

Love never gives up. Love cares more for others than for self. Love doesn't want what it doesn't have. Love doesn't strut, doesn't have a swelled head, doesn't force itself on others, isn't always "me first," doesn't fly off the handle, doesn't keep score of the sins of others, doesn't revel when others grovel, takes pleasure in the flowering of the truth, puts up with anything, trusts God always, always looks for the best, never looks back, but keeps going to the end.
　　—1 CORINTHIANS 13:4–7, THE MESSAGE

Heart emotions express themselves without expecting anything in return.

A RENEWED MIND

Because God understands us so thoroughly, He has chosen to rule in our lives through our new heart. When He established a covenant relationship with Israel (through Moses), He did it through circumcision—a cutting of the flesh, which drew blood.

When God began to teach us the spiritual implications behind this physical act of circumcision, He taught us about the circumcision of the heart.

Believers should not see things as "natural" people do. We should see things as God sees them, because we are looking through the eyes of our new heart.

God could not establish a covenant relationship with us through the brain. The love and obedience that flow from our brains are conditional—dependent upon "what's in it for me!" But the new heart says, "I will love you . . . obey you . . . care for you even if you will not respond to me. I will, in spite of what I see from you. I will, regardless of the way you treat me . . . I am still able to love you."

The brain gathers all of the facts, information and emotions. Then it rationalizes or reasons them out. When it gets through calculating, it says, "I like you, for now." The new heart (which comes from our Father) looks at everything, but because it is eternal, it sees beyond who a person is now to what he is going to become—and loves him until he gets there. This can only be done when you are equipped with knowledge that is beyond this earth. Believers should not see things as "natural" people do. We should see things as God sees them, because we are looking through the eyes of our new heart.

Without the governing influence of the new heart, we can fall prey to negative emotions like fear, anger, blame or insecurity. When this heart comes into a person's body, that person begins to see with a new perspective, even if he or she does not understand why. When we have a new heart, we learn to respond instead of react. For example, if someone offends you, the *natural* reaction would be anger because the emotion would be charged by the natural thought pattern. But a mind that has been renewed according to the Word can look at an offense and call it a blessing. The renewed mind is powerful.

Do not be conformed to this world (this age), [fashioned after and adapted to its external, superficial customs], but be transformed (changed) by the [entire] renewal of your mind [by its new ideals and its new attitude], so that you may prove [for yourselves] what is the good and acceptable and perfect will of God, even the thing which is good and acceptable and perfect [in His sight for you].

—ROMANS 12:2

When we have a new heart, we learn to respond instead of react.

SPEAKING FROM THE HEART

Sometimes when a person is in the physical healing process, a doctor will say, "She's fighting . . ." The person may have been wounded by a gunshot and may have all the probable signs indicating death. Yet in spite of the injury, the doctor says, " . . . but she's fighting."

That person's mind is saying, "I know that I am shot. I know that I am bleeding to death, but I am fighting to live." Very often it is the mind's response to an incident that determines the outcome.

Whatever your heart is full of is what your mouth is going to speak. When you say, "I am saved," it is because your heart is full, overflowing with abundance and salvation.

The same is true spiritually. When the heart and brain are out of alignment (resulting in an unrenewed mind), the thought patterns that are released into the world by way of the flesh will always be negative. This deceptive thinking can mean the difference between life and death.

Your new heart is already equipped with the ability to believe God. It comes "built with faith." The mind must learn to demonstrate, on every level, what the heart believes. A powerful confidence flows out of the new heart, a confidence Jesus demonstrated when He came into the world.

Jesus said confidently, "I am the door . . . I am the way . . . I am the resurrection." He did not say, "I *think* I am the door . . . I *think* I am the way . . . I *think* I am the resurrection." And if Jesus Christ, indeed, is the Word "made flesh" that has dwelled among us—and now the Word lives inside us—we can now make the same confessions. Confidently we can declare, "I am healed; I am delivered; I am set free!" If I believe "unto salvation," then this is how I am able to say that I am saved. God knows when He is alive and well inside us.

The Bible says, "Out of the abundance of the heart the mouth speaketh" (Matt. 12:34, KJV). Whatever your heart is full of . . . whatever overflows from it . . . is what your mouth is going to speak. When you say, "I am saved," it is because your heart is full, overflowing with abundance and salvation.

It's your heart, not the dictionary, that gives meaning to your words. A good person produces good deeds and words season after season. An evil person is a blight on the orchard.

—MATTHEW 12:34–35, THE MESSAGE

Your new heart is already equipped with the ability to believe God.

HEART WISDOM

Heart wisdom is very different from the wisdom of the mind. It is a wisdom only available to those who have received the new heart.

God is teaching us that we cannot grab hold of God—or of the knowledge and wisdom that is God's alone—with our natural minds. To understand God we must receive the new heart. In Joel 2:13 God tells us the only way to receive this new heart. We must "rend [our] hearts and not [our] garments and return to the Lord."

> The mind of Christ is the mind of the Word! God has given us the Bible literally to "possess" His mind— the mind of Christ— the Word made flesh.

This wisdom that comes from our new heart is available only to those who possess the Holy Spirit. The Holy Spirit does not baptize our mind! We receive the baptism of the Holy Spirit in our hearts, and when this happens, God teaches and trains us how to combine the spiritual "deposit" with the new, spiritual language.

The mind of Christ is the mind of the Word! God has given us the Bible literally to "possess" His mind—the mind of Christ—the Word made flesh. Once we possess His mind, we "do hold the thoughts (feelings [emotions!] and purposes) of His heart" (1 Cor. 2:16).

Spirit can be known only by spirit—God's Spirit and our spirits in open communion. Spiritually alive, we have access to everything God's Spirit is doing.
　　—1 CORINTHIANS 2:14–15, THE MESSAGE

This wisdom that comes from our new heart is available only to those who possess the Holy Spirit.

WALKING THE WALK

We will be tested in the fire of our daily living. The enemy will throw his fiery darts at us. But the fire does not come to harm us—it comes to appraise us. It is in the crucible of God's fire of testing that the evidence of our new heart begins to shine forth. It is as though God is saying, "Just checking to see if My heart is still in there. Just checking to see if My blood is still running through your veins."

The fire will reveal whether your heart is made of gold, silver and precious stones— the new heart—or if it is composed of hay, wood, stubble or straw— the old heart.

We will be tested. This is God's "checks-and-balance" way of seeing what rules in our lives. Is it your mind or your heart? I believe the test determines which part of you is in control. Do the thought patterns of your mind, which say "Fight back," "Be jealous" or "Be envious," determine your response? If so, you have reacted from your flesh and have sown to the fleshly realm, which is your mind, soul and body.

Or does your new heart overrule the old thought patterns? If your new heart controls your response, you have come out of the fire walking in the Spirit. You are truly minding the things of the Spirit.

After an intense testing, Job looked at his own righteousness and said, "Behold, I am of small account and vile!...I had heard of You [only] by the hearing of the ear, but now my [spiritual] eye sees You. Therefore I loathe [my words] and abhor myself and repent in dust and ashes" (Job 40:4; 42:5–6).

Through the fires of affliction, Job received the wisdom of his new heart, and it renewed his mind. Then he knew: Though he had lived uprightly before God, he didn't have a new heart. The fires of affliction revealed it. Repentance brought him out. And God, who is holy, just and altogether righteous, gave Job a double-portion of everything he had lost.

Can you endure the testing? Will you listen to the wisdom of your new heart?

The Spirit, not content to flit around on the surface, dives into the depths of God, and brings out what God planned all along.

—1 CORINTHIANS 2:10, THE MESSAGE

It is in the crucible of God's fire of testing that the evidence of our new heart begins to shine forth.

MATTERS

SECTION

OF THE

TEN

HEART

Devotions for Women

CARING FOR THE NEW HEART

THE NEW HEART

CRAVES WHAT GOD CRAVES,

LOVES WHAT HE LOVES

AND HATES WHAT HE HATES.

MEDITATE ON THE WORD

*I*f you simply read the Word, it will travel through the first, second and third regions of your mind. In order for it to penetrate the fourth center, the frontal lobes, you have to *meditate* on the Word—consistently keep it there until it permeates the fourth realm of decision. Then, as you study the Word, it will travel down your nerve endings and cause your body functions to relax and line up with the will of God.

As you keep putting the Word inside you, it will pierce through to the subconscious level and begin to heal your emotional memories.

As you keep putting the Word inside you, it will pierce through to the subconscious level and begin to heal your emotional memories. Then you will be able to stop comparing against negative, *emotionally familiar* experiences. As the Word pierces the depths of your mind, it will compare and replace these old memories according to the Word of God. You will gain a new perspective—one that will amaze you. Instead of being tormented by your old mind, you will be able to say, "No, I want the Word."

You have to keep meditating on the Word day and night (Ps. 1:2). Digest the Word over and over again until it gets through the cerebral cortex where you think, strategize, plan, reflect and become inspired as God takes your vision for the future to an incredible, new level. Then your imagination takes over from there, and you start seeing yourself succeed and prosper—until you have become an overcomer! As you consistently meditate on the Word, it will go to the frontal lobes, where the power of your decision will declare, "As for me and my house, we are going to live for God!"

I believe that when you receive the new heart, its power breaks the shackles of things that possessed you as a sinner (things that you hated and denounced). Yet there are still things that you love and do not want to release. Then it becomes the power of your decision to surrender those things to the Lord, which is done during your mind's renewing process.

You thrill to God's Word, you chew on Scripture day and night. You're a tree replanted in Eden, bearing fresh fruit every month, never dropping a leaf, always in blossom.
—PSALM 1:2–3, THE MESSAGE

You have to keep meditating on the Word day and night.

STEPS TO DELIVERANCE

The medulla, which contains the nerve centers that regulate breathing, heart rate and other body functions, starts to regulate and balance at conversion. The second stage involves the amygdala (storehouse of emotional memory) comparing the new information with what your emotions have already experienced. There has to be a showdown between the new heart and the old mind, which is where your internal battle begins.

When you begin to read the Word of God, the pressure waves from your new heart become so powerful that your heart rejects what is stored in your mind (in the amygdala). The warfare that comes back to the mind is so powerful that it causes you to get in the Word to see what the Bible says about it. When that Word comes in contact with your emotional memories, it begins to replace them with the new, sanctified thought pattern from your new heart.

Now your new heart is refusing to give up, because it cannot be overthrown. It is, after all, the heart of God. So it presses through to the third realm, the cerebral cortex, where it thinks, strategizes, reasons, plans and inspires, using the Word to inspire

> *When you begin to read the Word of God, the pressure waves from your new heart become so powerful that your heart rejects what is stored in your mind.*

the mind! It dissects the Word in order to strategize how you are going to keep your mind stayed on God.

This reaches the frontal lobes, which are involved in decision making. The lobes then send waves back to the amygdala to reflect the appropriate emotional response.

Your new heart exerts pressure on the old brain to receive and digest the Word. It goes completely through all four stages. By the time the Word reaches the decision-making center, it has rejected the memory and inspired the mind. After the decision is followed through, the body begins to line up in sync with the new heart rhythms that have passed through the frontal lobes back to the amygdala. This completed process is transmitted back to your physical being through the medulla as it pierces the subconscious level.

Which stage of mind renewal describes where you are today? Is your mind being renewed? Have you embraced your new heart?

How can a young person live a clean life? By carefully reading the map of your Word. I'm single-minded in pursuit of you; don't let me miss the road signs you've posted. I've banked my promises in the vault of my heart so I won't sin.
—PSALM 119:10–11, THE MESSAGE

Are you working out your own salvation with fear and trembling before God?

A PASSION FOR THE SPIRIT

A new heart comes with many godly attributes, including a strong conviction of what it believes. After all, God already "believes, accepts and receives" Himself. He has every confidence that His Word is true. He knows it will accomplish His divine purpose. We fall into error when we think of ourselves "more highly" than we should and then fail to trust and obey God.

Many in the church do not have the mind of Christ, so they live in a perpetual state of sin, saying, "I do not feel convicted about this. I do not feel bad about that." Their consciences have become darkened, and they habitually do things that displease God. They do not love God or fear Him unto obedience.

If this describes you, then I am sorry. You do not have the new heart.

When you have the new heart—God's heart—and you do anything that is contrary to God's Word, it will automatically send a wave of conviction. And because you love and fear God and believe in His name, you will repent.

There is a penalty for sin, one way or the other. If you habitually do things that are ungodly and sense no conviction, but just

When you have the new heart—God's heart—and you do anything that is contrary to God's Word, it will automatically send a wave of conviction.

say, "God understands," the old heart has deceived you. You are walking out a death sentence. If you can continue in a pattern of sin, you have not received the new heart. The new heart changes you completely, even if you cannot explain it. You cannot "coin" the new birth experience any more than a person can explain exactly what happens when he has undergone a heart transplant.

When we receive God's heart, it should birth a passion within us for holiness, worship and everything that pleases Him. It should automatically reject anything that does not sound, look, taste or feel like God. If it does not do this, something is wrong.

The Word says that we have been made "the righteousness of God in him" (2 Cor. 5:21, KJV). Don't reject the new heart's call to this righteousness!

Everyone who makes a practice of doing evil, addicted to denial and illusion, hates God-light and won't come near it, fearing a painful exposure. But anyone working and living in truth and reality welcomes God-light so the work can be seen for the God-work it is.

—JOHN 3:20–21, THE MESSAGE

If you can continue in a pattern of sin, you have not received the new heart.

THE DANGER OF HABITUAL SIN

When you reject the Word and do not put it into your heart and mind, the old nature assumes control—and you shut down the power and the activity of your new heart. God will not stay in this temple. You will have forced the Holy Spirit to leave, and not because you have done "one little thing" wrong. He will have left because you have refused to store the Word of God in your mind, enabling it to progress through all four stages of deliverance. You have refused to meditate on the Word. Therefore, your "emotional memories" and the stubbornness of your old mind can draw your heart to do something that offends God.

Anyone can make a mistake. But when ungodly behavior becomes habitual to the point that you no longer sense the heart's conviction, the new heart has been repelled.

Anyone can make a mistake. Falling into temptation and sin does not mean that you are not saved. But when ungodly behavior becomes habitual to the point that you no longer sense the heart's conviction, the new heart has been repelled. Because you have ignored the new heart's correction—deliberately annihilating its message, which says that you no longer desire God—you have rejected your new heart. When you consistently refuse the new heart's direction, you are sending a signal back saying, "I do not want you here." And the Spirit of the Lord will never stay where He is not wanted.

For the soil which has drunk the rain that repeatedly falls upon it and produces vegetation useful to those for whose benefit it is cultivated partakes of a blessing from God. But if [that same soil] persistently bears thorns and thistles, it is considered worthless and near to being cursed, whose end is to be burned.

—HEBREWS 6:7–8

The Spirit of the Lord will never stay where He is not wanted.

STAY SENSITIVE TO THE NEW HEART

If you allow your flesh (mind) to lead you into sin, and then you repent, God is just and able to forgive you. Why? You have been overtaken in a fault. You have been overtaken by memories of the brain. Man looks on the outside, but God sees your heart (1 Sam. 16:7). He knows that sin action did not come from your heart. It cropped up from your emotional memories. This is why it is critical for you to renew your mind.

Many people are still saying, "I am saved," as they willfully and continually do things that displease God.

When God turns someone over to a "reprobate" mind, more often than not it is someone who has declared that he has a new heart. Although that person receives convicting messages from God, he ignores them . . . continuously. His actions become a mockery against God. And God has no other choice but to turn that person over to a reprobate mind.

This is the danger that faces the church today. Many people are still saying, "I am saved," as they willfully and continually do things that displease God. That offends Him, to the point that He turns them over to a deceived and debased mind. This kind of mind is "deceitful . . . perverse . . . corrupt . . . and severely, mortally sick."

It would be better for these people to say, "I was saved, but I am in a backslidden state right now. I need prayer. My memories remind me what it felt like to be in an adulterous situation, and I just cannot say *no* to my brain waves. The memory is too strong. I cannot overthrow it." There is grace and mercy for these individuals. But when you have a new heart (that constantly sends waves of conviction), and you constantly reject the conviction while declaring how righteous and holy you are, the Spirit of the Lord will leave. Beloved, stay sensitive to the leading of the new heart!

Don't fool yourself into thinking that you are a listener when you are anything but, letting the Word go in one ear and out the other. Act on what you hear! Those who hear and don't act are like those who glance in the mirror, walk away, and two minutes later have no idea who they are, what they look like.

—James 1:23–24, The Message

 Stay sensitive to the leading of the new heart!

THE EVIL HEART

When we have the new heart and are studying the Word consistently, we have the ability to "squeeze out" ungodly thought patterns. But if we refuse to accept the directions of God's Word and act upon that evil thought, God has no alternative but to leave. He cannot dwell in the same place as sin.

When you backslide, you are in imminent danger. Your latter state becomes worse than your original state before receiving the new heart.

This puts you in imminent danger. When you backslide, your latter state becomes worse than your original state before receiving the new heart. Therefore, you will begin to experience the depths of the evil realm, which is worse than you have ever dreamed. Hear me. If you have followed the command of Joel 2:12–13 to rip out your old heart, and God has given you a new heart according to Ezekiel 11:19–20, and yet you reject that new heart, you will not merely revert back to the old heart that you had before.

When you "rend your heart" and give it to God, do you think that He puts it in a bank account and saves it? Do you think that He puts it in cold storage, saying, "I will save it just in case you do not want Me later?" No! He destroys it, just like anything else that looks like death. The destiny of that old heart is death and destruction, and since He came to give us everlasting, abundant life, He destroys anything that resembles death.

When you reject God, Satan brings you an evil heart, and you do not know what is in that heart, either. It is even more deceitful, because it "looks like" it is in perfect order—until it begins its evil transformation. And like the first heart transplant, your evil heart will not be connected to your mind. It will not obey either you or God.

This ought to make you hold on to God even if you have to fight tooth and nail! This knowledge should make you determined to put your old mind to death. It should make you feed your mind with the Word of God every day, because you do not ever want to backslide.

When the strong man, fully armed, [from his courtyard] guards his own dwelling, his belongings are undisturbed [his property is at peace and is secure]. But when one stronger than he attacks him and conquers him, he robs him of his whole armor on which he had relied and divides up and distributes all his goods as plunder (spoil). He who is not with Me [siding and believing with Me] is against Me, and he who does not gather with Me [engage in My interest], scatters.

—LUKE 11:21–23

Hold on to God even if you have to fight tooth and nail!

THE TIME FOR CHANGE HAS COME!

God is saying, loud and clear, that if we intend to live throughout eternity—if we intend to live for Him in this world—we need to change. If we don't, we will have massive heart failure and die a spiritual death. This is definitely a matter of the heart. Proverbs 4:23 says, "Keep and guard your heart with all vigilance and above all that you guard, for out of it flow the springs of life."

We must be vigilant, constantly examining our own hearts. Otherwise, we will continue to be the "great pretenders."

We must be vigilant, constantly examining our own hearts. Otherwise, we will continue to be the "great pretenders." One day the Lord may say to us, "Begone from Me...I never knew you" (Matt. 25:41; 7:23).

The Word of the Lord speaks to us from Revelation 2:5:

Remember then from what heights you have fallen. Repent (change the inner man to meet God's will) and do the works you did previously [when first you knew the Lord].

Heed this warning to care for your new heart diligently! God will be with us if we trust and obey our new heart. Above anything else, we must know that we have it, and then we must follow what it tells us to do.

But you walked away from your first love—why? What's going on with you, anyway? Do you have any idea how far you've fallen? A Lucifer fall! Turn back! Recover your dear early love. No time to waste, for I'm well on my way to removing your light from the golden circle.
—REVELATION 2:4–5, THE MESSAGE

Heed this warning to care for your new heart diligently!

MATTERS
OF THE
HEART

SECTION

ELEVEN

Devotions for Women

PRAYER AND THE NEW HEART

THE MORE YOU SEEK GOD,

THE DEEPER THE COUNSEL

WILL BECOME,

AND THE MORE

"SECRETS" HE WILL REVEAL.

KEYS OF THE KINGDOM

We know the problem, we have read the prophetic word, and we have examined the depths of the heart and mind. Now it's time to put what we know into practice. It's time to take the keys of God's Word and, from the deep chambers of our hearts, unshackle our minds—and ultimately the world—from the enemy's bondage. Remember what Jesus said in Matthew 16:19:

> *We are to "bind" what God has already bound in His Word and to "loose" what He has already loosed.*

> I will give you the keys of the kingdom of heaven; and whatever you bind (declare to be improper and unlawful) on earth must be what is already bound in heaven; and whatever you loose (declare lawful) on earth must be what is already loosed in heaven.

We are to "bind" what God has already bound in His Word and to "loose" what He has already loosed. We are not supposed to bind and loose what we desire or anything that has not first been revealed to us by God. If we have received the new heart, both heart and mind should be totally submitted to God's Word and ways. This is how we begin to experience and walk in the "counsel" of God.

And I tell you, you are Peter [Greek, Petros—a large piece of rock], and on this rock [Greek, petra—a huge rock like Gibraltar] I will build My church, and the gates of Hades (the powers of the infernal region) shall not overpower it [or be strong to its detriment or hold out against it].
—MATTHEW 16:18

It's time to put what we know into practice.

ESTABLISHING NEW HABITS

God is saying that we are to break old, fleshly habits and build a new habit of meditating on His Word...day and night. Let me bring this down to earth. It takes about twenty-one days to establish a new habit in your mind. So why don't you challenge yourself—for the next twenty-one days—to study and ponder the Word of God day and night? You will get results...and your battle will be won. When Daniel sought God for a message, the angel appeared and told him that his prayer had been heard but delayed for twenty-one days.

If you want to change, you have to "sow to the Spirit," consistently and persistently, to complete the transformation according to God's Word.

This could not be a coincidence! If you want to change, you have to "sow to the Spirit," consistently and persistently, to complete the transformation according to God's Word. That is when understanding comes. This is what God is after. This is what God wants to "unlock" through your new heart in order to renew your mind.

From the moment you decided to humble yourself to receive understanding, your prayer was heard, and I set out to come to you. But I was waylaid by the angel-prince of the kingdom of Persia and was delayed for a good three weeks. But then Michael, one of the chief angel-princes, intervened to help me . . . And now I'm here to help you understand what will eventually happen to your people.
—DANIEL 10:12–14, THE MESSAGE

Challenge yourself—for the next twenty-one days—to study and ponder the Word of God day and night.

SECRETS OF THE WORD

In Hebrews 4:12 we discover that an understanding of God's Word is released through our heart, which pierces the brain waves and flows through our emotions to transform our thoughts, plans and imagination. We read:

When you hear the voice of God in prayer, He will either speak to you through His Word (using His Word) or by speaking in harmony with what He has already revealed.

For the Word that God speaks is alive and full of power [making it active, operative, energizing, and effective]; it is sharper than any two-edged sword, penetrating to the dividing line of the breath of life (soul) and [the immortal] spirit, and of joints and marrow [of the deepest parts of our nature], exposing and sifting and analyzing and judging the very thoughts and purposes of the heart.

When you hear the voice of God in prayer, He will either speak to you through His Word (using His Word) or by speaking in harmony with what He has already revealed. The more you seek God, the deeper His counsel will become, and the more "secrets" He will reveal. You will gain more and more understanding.

If any of you is deficient in wisdom, let him ask of the giving God [Who gives] to everyone liberally and ungrudgingly, without reproaching or faultfinding, and it will be given him.
—JAMES 1:5

The more you seek God, the deeper His counsel will become, and the more "secrets" He will reveal.

OBEY THE WORD

When you decide to obey the Word, your brain waves flow back through your emotions into the depths of your subconscious mind and then to your body. The transformation is complete: soul, spirit, joints and marrow.

When you test out an option and determine that it is according to the Word of God, it is time to obey it with all of your heart.

Being double-minded is a state of conflict between the "brain of the heart" and the brain in your head. It is spiritual schizophrenia! It is proof that your new heart is still fighting for the victory. So how do you identify the wisdom that comes from God?

According to James, it is "first of all pure (undefiled); then it is peace-loving, courteous (considerate, gentle). [It is willing to] yield to reason, full of compassion and good fruits; it is whole-hearted and straight-forward, impartial and unfeigned (free from doubts, wavering, and insincerity)" (James 3:17). When you test out an option and determine that it is according to the Word of God, it is time to obey it with all of your heart.

Only it must be in faith that he asks with no wavering (no hesitating, no doubting). For the one who wavers (hesitates, doubts) is like the billowing surge at sea that is blown hither and thither and tossed by the wind. For truly, let not such a person imagine that he will receive anything [he asks for] from the Lord. [For being as he is] a man of two minds (hesitating, dubious, irresolute), [he is] unstable and unreliable and uncertain about everything [he thinks, feels, decides].

—JAMES 1:6–8

Being double-minded is a state of conflict between the "brain of the heart" and the brain in your head. It is spiritual schizophrenia!

THE FATHER'S WISDOM

When you respond to your new heart, obeying its "intelligent communication" so that the Word penetrates your mind and brings your body into subjection to God's Word, you have won the victory. And once you have gained the victory of the new heart, you can consistently receive and respond to the undefiled wisdom of our Father. He can trust you with His secrets.

If you are living in sin, the only thing that God will likely tell you is to repent. Once you have repented from habitual sin, you can then receive the "deep, inner" meaning of His heavenly counsel.

> *Sometimes you will receive wisdom in prayer that conflicts with everything you see and feel, but it covers you like a warm blanket. This is the wisdom of God.*

Sometimes you will receive wisdom in prayer that conflicts with everything you see and feel, but it covers you like a warm blanket. This is the wisdom of God. As you go deeper in God, He will begin to lead you in everything you do. He will give you intercessory "assignments" and tell you what to pray according to His Word. Other times, He will lead you to lie silently at the altar or to dance and sing before Him. The most important thing is to do what He leads you to do and to remember what He has already said.

God wants to "heal [our] land" (2 Chron. 7:14). He longs to

deliver us from the problem that has emerged from our old, deceitful hearts (Jer. 17:9). We must receive the new heart and begin to seek God while He can still be found. We must forsake our own thoughts and put on the humble mind of Christ. (See Philippians 2:5–8.) Then, and only then, will God release true "prosperity." And it will not only heal us; it will heal our land.

From now on every road you travel will take you to God.
Follow the Covenant signs; read the charted directions...
God-friendship is for God-worshipers; they are the ones he
confides in.
—PSALM 25:10, 14, THE MESSAGE

When you respond to your new heart, obeying its "intelligent communication" so that the Word penetrates your mind and brings your body into subjection to God's Word, you have won the victory.

PRAISE AND PETITION

Before you can begin to pray effectively, you need to understand exactly what prayer is, so let us begin with praise and petition. Yes, I started with praise, and, yes, it works together with petition! You enter God's presence through your praises, because thanking God proves your faith in Him to perform His Word. After all, if you do not believe that God answers prayer, you might as well not even ask—because He does not answer "double-minded" requests.

> *If you do not believe that God answers prayer, you might as well not even ask.*

Do not fret or have any anxiety about anything, but in every circumstance and in everything, by prayer and petition (definite requests), with thanksgiving, continue to make your wants known to God. And God's peace [shall be yours, that tranquil state of a soul assured of its salvation through Christ, and so fearing nothing from God and being content with its earthly lot of whatever sort that is, that peace] which transcends all understanding shall garrison and mount guard over your hearts and minds in Christ Jesus.

—PHILIPPIANS 4:6–7

You enter God's presence through your praises, because thanking God proves your faith in Him to perform His Word.

THE PRAYER OF CONSECRATION

There is an intensified prayer of consecration where you press into God with a need to know and do God's will—not your own. It is where you are separated from earthly cares to embrace His higher, eternal purpose. And it is also where eternal life is released.

In the prayer of consecration, you sacrifice yourself at the altar of God's will.

Jesus said, "Unless a grain of wheat falls into the earth and dies, it remains [just one grain; it never becomes more but lives] by itself alone. But if it dies, it produces many others and yields a rich harvest" (John 12:24). He knew this as He prayed alone in Gethsemane while the disciples slept. He knew one day they would receive a new heart.

Going a little ahead, he fell on his face, praying, "My Father, if there is any way, get me out of this. But please, not what I want. You, what do you want?"
—MATTHEW 26:39, THE MESSAGE

By faith, this woman went to her spiritual authority and called those things that were not as though they were. She already knew what "was not," because nobody else had been able to heal her daughter. Yet her heart cried out, and it moved her beyond her natural mind. She pressed into Jesus with an urgent need and got His attention. He granted her prayer of faith—instantly.

Are you hurting? Pray . . . Are you sick? Call the church leaders together to pray and anoint you with oil in the name of the Master. Believing-prayer will heal you, and Jesus will put you on your feet.
     —JAMES 5:13–15, THE MESSAGE

What is your heart's cry to Jesus? The prayer of faith can release it, because God cares for you.

THE PRAYER OF AGREEMENT

The prayer of agreement is joining your faith with two or three others before God. Jesus did this when He raised Lazarus from the dead in John 11. He told His disciples, "And for your sake I am glad that I was not there; it will help you to believe (to trust and rely on Me)" (v. 15). When Jesus arrived in Bethany, Martha said, "Master, if You had been here, my brother would not have died. And even now I know that whatever You ask from God, He will grant it to You" (vv. 21–22).

In the prayer of agreement, you can overcome spiritual strongholds by joining in faith with someone else. The strongholds have to come down!

Right then, Jesus found a point of identification in Martha. In verses 25–27, He said:

I am [Myself] the Resurrection and the Life. Whoever believes in (adheres to, trusts in, and relies on) Me, although he may die, yet he shall live; and whoever continues to live and believes in (has faith in, cleaves to, and relies on) Me shall never [actually] die at all. Do you believe this?

She said to Him, Yes, Lord, I have believed [I do believe] that You are the Christ (the Messiah, the Anointed One), the Son of God, [even He] Who was to come into the world.

Then Jesus wept when Mary and the others came, not believing (vv. 32–28). But it didn't matter. Unbelief had already been bound by the power of agreement. He told them to roll away the stone...and Martha cried out, "But Lord, by this time he [is decaying and] throws off an offensive odor...Jesus said to her, Did I not tell you and promise you that if you would believe and rely on Me, you would see the glory of God?" (vv. 39–40).

Lazarus came forth—even though many there did not believe. You see, his death sentence was pronounced by Satan, but Deuteronomy 19:15 had already declared: "One witness shall not prevail against a man...only on the testimony of two or three witnesses shall a charge be established." It is also the way a charge or curse can definitely be broken.

Jesus knew that. And so should we.

When two of you get together on anything at all on earth and make a prayer of it, my Father in heaven goes into action. And when two or three of you are together because of me, you can be sure that I'll be there.

—MATTHEW 18:19–20, THE MESSAGE

If you continue believing and relying on Jesus, you will see the glory of God.

THE PRAYER OF INTERCESSION

Intercession is when you pray the burden of the Lord for others. And God covers you, because He has led you to that place. James 5:16 says, "The earnest (heartfelt, continued) prayer of a righteous man makes tremendous power available [dynamic in its working]." This means God has to consecrate you to be an intercessor. You can't just up and decide to do it.

In the prayer of intercession, you pray the burden of the Lord for others.

You personally have to come through each level of prayer in the outer court: the gate (salvation and thanksgiving), the brazen laver (washing/cleansing) and the brazen altar (purification/sanctification). Then you can put on your priestly garments and enter the place of divine service—the holy place—where the fires of intercession burn continually on the golden altar.

By now, God has found a point of identification in you—because you have literally been clothed in His righteousness. Everything you are wearing matches the colors and patterns in the tabernacle. You are now ready to receive the Lord's burden and faithfully bring it to Him in intercession until His purpose is released in that matter.

Again, it's all about the heart, because when God measures the change in you, He sees a heart that is more like His. And that heart can change the world.

The first thing I want you to do is pray. Pray every way you know how, for everyone you know.
      —1 TIMOTHY 2:1, THE MESSAGE

God has to consecrate you—take you through every level of prayer—to make you an effective intercessor.

ASKING, SEEKING AND KNOCKING

The kingdom of God is like "something precious buried in a field" (Matt. 13:44). Because of this, there are increasing intensities of prayer: asking, seeking and knocking. Simply put, *to ask* is to petition God for your needs or to make intercession for the needs of others. *To seek* means to ask God for deeper wisdom and, at the same time, to search the Word for deeper insight. It can also mean that you study other resources or look more deeply into the things around you. In addition, seeking can mean that you receive godly counsel in order to get a full understanding of what God is saying.

As you pray, you must learn how to press in to God.

Knocking is pressing in further through persistent prayer, fasting and obedience to God's revealed and written Word.

Keep on asking and it will be given you; keep on seeking and you will find; keep on knocking [reverently] and [the door] will be opened to you. For everyone who keeps on ask-

ing receives; and he who keeps on seeking finds; and to him
who keeps on knocking, [the door] will be opened.
—MATTHEW 7:7–8

 Sometimes we have to dig deeper, wait longer and press in harder to get the full revelation.

THE POWER OF FASTING

When you fast, you willingly give up food and anything else that stands in God's way in order to hear God, obey Him and accomplish His purpose.

Fasting from food is extremely powerful because your new heart is bypassing your mind (which is bent on survival) and going directly to your body, which tells the brain, "Man shall not live and be upheld and sustained by bread alone, but by every word that comes forth from the mouth of God" (Matt. 4:4). To coin a phrase, fasting is "putting your body where your heart is" to squeeze out any form of mind control.

When you overcome in a fast, the devil has to flee; there is a clear path—within you and outside you—for God's will and purpose to be done.

This is also why it is good to meditate even more deeply on the Word during a fast. It escalates the two-pronged counterattack to an all-out, three-pronged assault against the enemy. In other words, denying yourself food can help you to see that other "earthly" things are not that important—which opens the door to obedience in every area of your life. Ecclesiastes 4:12 says, "A threefold cord is not quickly broken."

When you overcome in a fast, the devil has to flee; there is a clear path—within you and outside you—for God's will and purpose to be done. Let me say this a different way: When you overcome by denying yourself food, time, money, convenience and whatever you value most, the devil will not be able to tempt you because you have already rejected everything that he can throw in your direction. His tactics have been exposed. And he cannot stay in the light; he has to run from it because his evil deeds are immediately seen and exposed for what they truly are.

[Rather] is not this the fast that I have chosen; to loose the bonds of wickedness, to undo the bands of the yoke, to let the oppressed go free, and that you break every [enslaving] yoke? Is it not to divide your bread with the hungry and bring the homeless poor into your house—when you see the naked, that you cover him, and that you hide not yourself from [the needs of] your own flesh and blood? Then shall your light break forth like the morning, and your healing (your restoration and the power of a new life) shall spring forth speedily; your righteousness (your rightness, your justice, and your right relationship with God) shall go before you [conducting you to peace and prosperity], and the glory of the Lord shall be your rear guard.

—Isaiah 58:6–8

Fasting is "putting your body where your heart is" to squeeze out any form of mind control.

THE HEART OF PRAYER

Obviously, prayer is not what it needs to be in the body of Christ because we are operating from wicked, deceived hearts (Jer. 17:9). Prayer will be restored as we obey our new hearts and renew our old, stubborn minds. Today, in this season and final hour of the church, prayer will be the final test of any genuine believer or work for God.

> *Prayer is our vital connection to God through the vehicle of our new hearts. If we do not pray, we will not have the life of Christ within us.*

Prayer is our vital connection to God through the vehicle of our new hearts. If we do not pray, we will not have the life of Christ within us. We will be unproductive and, even worse, could be told on that Day, "I never knew you."

You must decide whether to hear and embrace this word of prophecy—and inherit eternal life—or to continue walking in your own thoughts and ways, and reap destruction. The choice is yours.

I pray and trust that you will choose to obey God and reap eternal life.

Dwell in Me, and I will dwell in you. [Live in Me, and I will live in you.] Just as no branch can bear fruit of itself without abiding in (being vitally united to) the vine, neither can you bear fruit unless you abide in Me. I am the Vine; you are the branches. Whoever lives in Me and I in him bears much (abundant) fruit. However, apart from Me [cut off from vital union with Me] you can do nothing. If a person does not dwell in Me, he is thrown out like a [broken-off] branch, and withers; such branches are gathered up and thrown into the fire, and they are burned. If you live in Me [abide vitally united to Me] and My words remain in you and continue to live in your hearts, ask whatever you will, and it shall be done for you.

—JOHN 15:4–7

Prayer will be restored as we obey our new hearts and renew our old, stubborn minds.

DAILY PRAYER

Prayer is something that must be practiced on a daily basis. I adapted this daily "prayer practice" from a powerful, in-depth teaching called "The Power of Positive Prayer Points" in Matthew Ashimolowo's special edition Bible.[10]

> *Start each day loving God and people. This means your relationship with God is good, and that as far as you are able, your relationships with family members, friends, coworkers and others are in line with the Word.*

- Start each day loving God and people. This means your relationship with God is good, and that as far as you are able, your relationships with family members, friends, coworkers and others are in line with the Word.
- Start each day communing with God through Bible study and prayer.
- Thank God, praise Him for answering your prayers and worship Him for who He is.
- Repent, asking God to forgive you and to cleanse your heart from every sin, known and unknown.
- Thank God for your spiritual armor, as listed in Ephesians 6:10–18.

- Surrender yourself to the Holy Spirit so He can pray through you, according to Romans 8:26–27.
- Be ready to obey the Holy Spirit's leading, to petition (for your needs) or intercede (for others); declare God's Word; lie still, or do whatever God leads you to do.
- Ask God to build a hedge of protection around your life, family and all others who are praying with you against the enemy's devices.
- Ask God to rebuke Satan and all his servants.
- Take authority over the enemy's work and his attempts to attack your new heart (spirit), your mind (emotions, logic and decision making) and body.

Repeat these steps until you know that you have broken through in the Spirit realm and that God is leading you in prayer and intercession.

Clean the slate, God, so we can start the day fresh! Keep me from stupid sins, from thinking I can take over your work; then I can start this day sun-washed, scrubbed clean of the grime of sin. These are the words in my mouth; these are what I chew on and pray. Accept them when I place them on the morning altar, O God, my Altar-Rock, God, Priest-of-My-Altar.

        —PSALM 19:12–14, THE MESSAGE

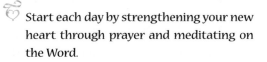

Start each day by strengthening your new heart through prayer and meditating on the Word.

NOTES

1. Doc Lew Childre and Howard Martin, *The HeartMath Solution* (San Francisco, CA: HarperSanFrancisco, 2000), 9.

2. Ibid., 33.

3. Paul Pearsall, *The Heart's Code* (New York: Broadway Books, 1998), 24–25.

4. Childre and Martin, *The HeartMath Solution*, 41.

5. Pearsall, *The Heart's Code*, 66.

6. Childre and Martin, *The HeartMath Solution*, 34.

7. Adapted from Childre and Martin, *The HeartMath Solution*, 31.

8. Elaine Farris Hughes, *Writing From the Inner Self* (New York: Harper Perennial, 1992), 4.

9. Childre and Martin, *The HeartMath Solution*. Also, source retrieved from the Internet: The High-Performance Mind and encyclopedia.com.

10. The Daily Prayer Practice was adapted from a special edition King James Bible by Matthew Ashimolowo, in a section titled, "The Power of Positive Prayer Points," page 17. For more information regarding this resource, contact Matthew Ashimolowo Media Ministries, London, England, or go to his website at www.kicc.org.uk.

THE MOST IMPORTANT

THING IS TO HAVE

A NEW HEART

AND TO KNOW—

YOU HAVE IT!

THIS WORD FROM THE LORD CHANGED JUANITA BYNUM'S LIFE... AND IT CAN CHANGE YOURS TOO!

We pray that these powerful words have impacted your life and that each day will bring about a transformation in your heart.

Juanita Bynum

Stop trying to fix the old—Let God give you something new

Over 300,000 copies sold!
CHARISMA HOUSE PUBLISHING

Matters of the *Heart*

Now you can dig a little deeper and explore the heart/mind connection and see why this key to intimacy with God is so vital to a healthy, satisfying and effective life.

0-88419-832-4
$13.99

323/DA3N00

Call 1-800-599-5750 to order this bestseller!
Visit our Web site at charismahouse.com to save even more.

Charisma HOUSE
A STRANG COMPANY
Everything good starts here!